● ● ● Supporting inclusion in
the early years

● ● ● Supporting inclusion in the early years

Caroline A. Jones

Open University Press
Maidenhead · New York

Open University Press
McGraw-Hill Education
McGraw-Hill House
Shoppenhangers Road
Maidenhead, Berkshire
England SL6 2QL

email: enquiries@openup.co.uk
world wide web: www.openup.co.uk

First published 2004

A catalogue record for this book is available from the British Library.

ISBN 0 335 210 910 (pb)   0 335 210 929 (hb)

Library of Congress Cataloging-in-Publication Data has been applied for

Typeset by YHT Ltd, London
Printed in Great Britain by Bell and Bain, Glasgow

Contents

Series editors' preface   vii
Acknowledgements   x

Introduction   1

1 Making exclusion visible: labels, language and attitudes   5

2 Early identification and assessment   21

3 A graduated model of assessment and provision   33

4 Developing inclusive policy and practice   52

5 The changing role of the special educational needs coordinator   72

6 Parents, children and professionals working together   86

7 Beyond the paintpots: inclusion and learning support assistants   101

Conclusion   112

Useful addresses   114
References   120
Index   126

Series editors' preface

This book is one of a series which will be of interest to all those who are concerned with the care and education of children from birth to 6 years' old – childminders, teachers and other professionals in schools, those who work in playgroups, private and community nurseries and similar institutions, governors, providers and managers. We also speak to parents and carers, whose involvement is probably the most influential of all for children's learning and development.

Our focus is on improving the effectiveness of early education. Policy developments come and go, and difficult decisions are often forced on all those with responsibility for young children's well-being. We aim to help with these decisions by showing how developmental approaches to young children's education not only accord with our fundamental educational principles, but provide a positive and sound basis for learning.

Each book recognizes and demonstrates that children from birth to 6 have particular developmental learning needs, and that all those providing care and education for them would be wise to approach their work developmentally. This applies just as much to the acquisition of subject knowledge, skills and understanding as to other educational goals such as social skills, attitudes and dispositions. In this series, there are several volumes with a subject-based focus, and the main aim is to show how that can be introduced to young children within the framework of an integrated and developmentally appropriate curriculum, without losing its integrity as an area of knowledge in its own right. We also stress the importance of providing a learning environment which is carefully planned for children's own active learning. Moreover, the present volume is especially concerned that this environment incorporates activities which *include all the children involved in a setting*. As the author emphasizes, 'support is based in the context of providing developmentally appropriate learning experiences in an inclusive environment which is planned to meet the needs of all children, *not only those perceived as having special educational needs*'.

Access for all children is fundamental to the provision of educational opportunity. We are concerned to emphasize antidiscriminatory approaches throughout, as well as the importance of recognizing that meeting special educational needs must be an integral purpose of curriculum development and planning. We see the role of play in learning as a central one, and one which also relates to all-round emotional, social and physical development. Play, along with other forms of active learning, is normally a natural point of access to the curriculum for each child at his or her particular stage and level of understanding. It is therefore an essential force in making for equal opportunities in learning, intrinsic as it is to all areas of development. We believe that these two aspects, play and equal opportunities, are so important that we not only highlight them in each volume in this series, but we also include separate volumes on them as well.

Throughout this series, we encourage readers to reflect on the education being offered to young children, by revisiting the developmental principles which most practitioners hold, and using them to analyse their observations of the children. In this way, readers can evaluate ideas about the most effective ways of educating young children, and develop strategies for approaching their practice in ways which exemplify their fundamental educational beliefs, and offer every child a more appropriate education.

The authors of each book in the series subscribe to the following set of principles for a developmental curriculum:

- Each child is an individual and should be respected and treated as such.
- The early years are a period of development in their own right, and the education of young children should be seen as a specialism with its own valid criteria of appropriate practice.
- The role of the educator of young children is to engage actively with what most concerns the child, and to support learning through these preoccupations.
- The educator has a responsibility to foster positive attitudes in

children to both self and others, and to counter negative messages which children may have received.

- Each child's cultural and linguistic endowment is seen as the fundamental medium of learning.
- An antidiscriminatory approach is the basis of all respect-worthy education, and is essential as a criterion for a developmentally appropriate curriculum (DAC).
- All children should be offered equal opportunities to progress and develop, and should have equal access to good-quality provision. The concepts of multiculturalism and antiracism are intrinsic to this whole educational approach.
- Partnership with parents should be given priority as the most effective means of ensuring coherence and continuity in children's experiences, and in the curriculum offered to them.
- A democratic perspective permeates education of good quality, and is the basis of transactions between people.

Vicky Hurst and Jenefer Joseph
Series editors

Acknowledgements

I would like to thank Shona Mullen of Open University Press, the original commissioning editor for this book, and more recently Fiona Richman for her patience, advice and support. I am grateful to Professor Geoff Lindsay at the University of Warwick for his comments on the draft chapters. Special thanks go to Warwickshire County Council Disability, Illness, Sensory and Communication Service (DISCS) for allowing me to incorporate their training materials and examples of good practice, especially Zoë Harwood, team leader and teacher for special educational needs (SEN) preschool and childcare, the SEN team and Dave Browne, senior manager of the service for their time. Thanks are due to Susan Clinton for work on the manuscript. I am indebted to all the staff at Pathways Childcare Centres, particularly Angie Norton and Sue Harris, for keeping the nurseries afloat while I became a 'part-time' boss. I would like to express my appreciation to my personal friends Audrey and Christine, for endless supportive phone conversations and for keeping me on target. Extra thanks to all the parents, teachers and children whose experiences I have used in this book. Finally, love and thanks to my two sons, Richard and Daniel, for giving me the time and space to complete this book.

Introduction

'Colin's going to a school for nutters and dumbos.'

It was this child's comment that sparked my interest in special education almost 20 years ago. As a student teacher, I was intrigued as to exactly where it was that 6-year-old 'Colin' was going, particularly as he was in my class and as far as I could see there was nothing wrong with him. Colin suffered from epilepsy and the school turned out to be a school for children with 'physical handicaps'. This chance encounter resulted in a visit to the special school, following which I was introduced to the special education community, a separate network of children and teachers I had never known existed. Ironically, this was in the year that the Warnock Report (DES 1978), a significant landmark in special education, was published, a report which stated that 'The purpose of education for all children is the same; the goals are the same. But the help individual children need in progressing towards them will be different' (para. 1.4). More recently, the idea of common goals for all young children has been endorsed in the *Curriculum Guidance for the Foundation Stage* (DfEE/QCA 2000) which established a framework of stepping stones towards 'early learning goals' encompassing children from their third birthday to the end of the reception class year. The guidance clearly stated that 'no child should be excluded or disadvantaged because of special educational needs, disability, or ability' (p. 11).

The *Special Educational Needs* (SEN) *Code of Practice* (DfES 2001a) recognizes a continuum of need and states as a fundamental principle that

SEN will normally be met in mainstream schools or early education settings. According to Section 313 (2) of the Education Act 1996, Section 4 (1) of the Grant Maintained Schools Act 1996 and Section 123 of the School Standards and Framework Act 1998 all early education providers in receipt of government funding are required to have regard to the *Code of Practice* (DfES 2001a). These include mainstream and special schools, maintained nursery schools, independent schools, non-maintained special schools, local authority daycare providers such as day nurseries and family centres, other registered full daycare and sessional care providers (e.g. preschools, playgroups, private day nurseries), plus Portage home teaching schemes and accredited childminders working as part of an approved network. The supporting criteria Standard 10 of the *National Standards for Under Eights Daycare and Childminding* (DfES 2001b) also states that the registered person should have regard to the *Code of Practice*. As a consequence, supporting SEN and inclusion in the early years is high on the early childhood agenda. However, it is important to recognize that our efforts are set against a changing and turbulent policy context.

Special education and early years education, both traditionally low-status areas in the national policy arena, have been subject to an intense and simultaneous burst of central government interest. This has resulted in an unprecedented number of policy documents and subsequent opportunities for changes in practice. The origins of the frantic pace of educational change in the UK can be traced back to the 1988 Education Reform Act and the introduction of the National Curriculum. The years of compulsory education were divided into four key stages with the earliest being Key Stage 1, incorporating 5- to 7-year-olds. A framework of statutory assessment was established at the end of each key stage. However, the School Curriculum and Assessment Authority (SCAA) recognized the importance of education in the early years if pupils were to make satisfactory progress in Key Stage 1. *Nursery Education: Desirable Outcomes for Children's Learning on Entering Compulsory Education* (SCAA 1996) heralded the first set of learning goals specifically intended for children of pre-compulsory school age in the private, voluntary and maintained sectors. Although not a statutory curriculum, preschool settings wishing to accept nursery voucher funding for the provision of nursery education were required to demonstrate, through inspection, how they promoted the desirable learning outcomes in six areas of learning. At this stage, the emphasis for the role of nursery education was on preparing children for the National Curriculum, rather than a balanced consideration of the child development perspective. The next major change was the introduction of compulsory baseline assessment for 5-year-olds from September 1998, bringing a whole new cohort of young children under the formal assessment umbrella. September 2000 brought the introduction of a 'foundation' stage, giving a distinct identity to this period of care and education of children aged 3 to the end of the reception year. The desirable learning outcomes were replaced by the *Curriculum Guidance for the Foundation Stage* (DfEE/QCA 2000) for early years settings which receive nursery grant funding and schools with nursery and reception-age children. This prompted the replacement of statutory baseline assessment by the *Foundation Stage Profile* (DfES 2003).

Meanwhile, the special education arena was undergoing equally dramatic changes. The 1993 Education Act required the secretary of state to issue a code of practice on the identification and assessment of children with SEN. The *Code* (DfE 1994) provided a common framework for all schools, local education authorities (LEAs) and others to follow in identifying, assessing and providing for children with perceived SEN. Separate guidance was issued for preschool settings outside the LEA-maintained sector wishing to redeem nursery education vouchers. In October 1997 the Green Paper, *Excellence for All Children: Meeting Special Educational Needs*, was described as 'the first step in a fundamental reappraisal of the way we meet special educational needs' (DfEE 1997a: 6). This was followed a year later by *Meeting Special Educational Needs: A Programme of Action* (DfEE 1998) which said that inclusion was the 'keystone' of government education policy. The Special Educational Needs and Disability Act (SENDA) was passed in 2001. In the same year, a revised SEN *Code of Practice* (DfES 2001a) superseded the original *Code* and came into effect from January 2002, forming a framework directed at identifying, assessing and providing for children with perceived SEN, as quickly and as early as possible. It states at the outset that LEAs should work with settings 'to ensure that any child's special educational needs are *identified early*' (para. 1.6, original emphasis).

The revised *Code* includes a whole new section dedicated to identification, assessment and provision in early education settings, including approved childminder networks. It is based upon these fundamental principles:

- a child with SEN should have their needs met;
- SEN will normally be met in mainstream schools or settings;
- the views of the child should be sought and taken into account;
- parents have a vital role to play in supporting their child's education;
- children with SEN should be offered full access to a broad, balanced and relevant education, including an appropriate curriculum for the foundation stage.

It is the role of those working or involved with young children to apply these principles which underpin the themes throughout this book. However, identifying, assessing and supporting children with SEN in the early years can be a complex process. Care must be taken to ensure that intentionally or otherwise, the graduated model of assessment and intervention, recommended in the *Code* (DfE 1994; DfES 2001a) does not simply create a 'spiral of separation' (Jones 2000), whereby increasing numbers of children are labelled and perceived as 'special' or somehow 'different' from the majority of their peer group at progressively earlier ages. When difficulties are seen to arise from the SEN of children it often follows that support is viewed as providing additional people to work with particular children. This book takes a broader view of support: as all the activities, planned and unplanned, which help those working with young children to respond to a range of learning needs. Support is based in the context of providing developmentally appropriate learning experiences in an inclusive environment which is planned to meet the needs of all children, not only those perceived as having SEN. The chapters that follow explore and discuss ways in which this can be achieved and attempt to fill the gap between rhetoric and reality.

Chapter 1 focuses on the language of SEN and suggests that a consideration of the concepts of inclusion, integration and SEN is essential in striving to develop 'inclusive education' in early childhood. It sets the stage for the development during the rest of the chapters of an interactive and inclusive model of supporting children with SEN in the early years. Chapter 2 raises issues around the notion of early identification and assessment, highlighting the dilemmas facing early education practitioners when deciding whether or not to identify children as having SEN. Chapter 3 focuses on the graduated model of intervention recommended in the *Code* (DfES 2001a) and on supporting children's learning through individual education plans (IEPs). It suggests that IEPs should be regarded as a natural part of the normal planning cycle – in other words, 'built in' rather than 'bolted on' to normal arrangements. Chapter 4 focuses on the development of inclusive policies. While acknowledging that supporting children with SEN in the early years is the concern of all early years practitioners, Chapter 5 discusses specific roles and responsibilities of the special educational needs coordinator (SENCO). Chapter 6 considers the notion of partnership with parents and uses the idea of an 'eternal triangle' of intervention (Jones 1998) to illustrate how parents, professionals and children are inextricably linked in meeting children's learning needs. The final chapter suggests that unless managed effectively, the role of the learning support assistant (LSA) in supporting a child with SEN can be counterproductive and lead to exclusive practice. Some useful addresses and an overall conclusion are then provided.

1

Making exclusion visible: labels, language and attitudes

> Whether backward children spend their early years in an infant school or in a special school, their education in the early stages should resemble that of a normal nursery group.
>
> (DES 1964: 56)

The language surrounding the development of special education is complex, confusing and liable to change (Tomlinson 1982). The labels given to children perceived as different from the majority of children the same age have changed over time. However, we need to be sure that the attitudes towards the labels have also changed. Numerous formal and informal labels have been assigned to children perceived as somehow different from other children of the same age (see Tables 1.1 and 1.2). As well as formal categories, an equally powerful informal labelling system prevails. In 1997, for example, an undergraduate student teacher reported in a seminar at the University of Warwick that in her teaching placement school the 'special needs' group were dubbed the 'CRAFT' group, an acronym for 'Can't Remember A F ...ing Thing'. Moreover, the labels and terms have different meanings according to the context in which they are used. It is important for those working with young children to acknowledge the complexity of the current label 'special educational needs' and question exactly what it means. The term was officially introduced into education policy in the 1981 Education Act, following a recommendation in the Warnock Report (DES 1978). This report, published following an extensive review of educational provision for handicapped children and young people, recommended replacing the statutory medical categories of handicap with an apparently relative and flexible concept of 'special educational need'. It envisaged a range of need and provision, suggesting that potentially as many as 20 per cent, or one in five children, would have SEN at some time in their school career, with 2 per cent being severe and complex. The overall result was that the child population defined as 'special' or different from the 'norm' was greatly expanded. Special education was extended in scope and officially became the concern of all schools, teachers and professionals working with children rather than the separate domain of a limited number of specialists.

The Warnock Report also highlighted the importance of early identification and assessment of children perceived as having difficulties. It suggested that if children were to get the help they needed they must be properly assessed, stating that a child's needs must be 'assessed as soon as possible so that appropriate help can be provided' (DES 1978: 4.26). However, even Baroness Warnock acknowledged that: 'The concept of "special need" carries a fake objectivity. For one of the main, indeed almost overwhelming, difficulties is to decide whose needs are special, and what "special" means' (Warnock 1982: 372).

Table 1.1 The numerous formal and informal labels assigned to children with SEN

Formal	Informal
Retarded	Idiot
Cripple	Thickie
Feeble minded	Spaz
Mentally defective	Drongo
Brain injured	Nutter
Educationally subnormal	Dumbo
Mongoloid	Stupid
Remedial	Daft
Ineducable	Dunce
Backward	
Maladjusted	
Handicapped	
Dull	
Exceptional	
Wheelchair bound	
Spastic	
Slow learner	
Imbecile	

Table 1.2 Official categories and labels

Code of Practice 1994	Code of Practice 2001
Learning difficulties	Communication and interaction
Specific learning difficulties	Cognition and learning
Emotional and behavioural difficulties	Behaviour, emotional and social development
Physical disabilities	Sensory and/or physical
Sensory impairment/hearing	
Sensory impairment/visual	
Speech and language difficulties	
Medical conditions	

The rest of this chapter explores ways in which the key terms 'SEN', 'integration' and 'inclusion' are interpreted in policy and practice. It argues that consideration of the language of SEN is crucial in striving to develop effective inclusive education in early childhood.

It is important for early years practitioners to consider the helpfulness of maintaining the division between 'normal' and 'special' children in terms of meeting their learning and developmental needs. We need to examine the rhetoric and practice of 'inclusion' as distinct from the more familiar term 'integration', a term traditionally associated with the placement of 'handicapped' children alongside their peers in mainstream educational settings. We also need to pay attention to the importance of external factors in creating or exacerbating SEN as well as in supporting inclusion. In other words, it is essential to place inclusive early childhood education within the context of effective early education for all children, not only those perceived to have SEN. Unless the curriculum, pedagogy and management structures of early years educational settings are challenged and changed, then their disabling potential is ignored (Vincent *et al.* 1996). Only by highlighting exclusionary pressures and suggesting ways in which early years workers can identify and begin to remove barriers to inclusion in early education settings can we begin to move forward.

The complexity of SEN

The Warnock Report (DES 1978) intended to set out a framework for a redirection of special education policy away from systems traditionally based on categorization and segregation towards more flexible arrangements. It appeared to represent a radical change in the way in which provision for pupils with SEN was considered. Significantly, the Report was the first official government document to emphasize provision for the handicapped preschool child, considering this as neglected and a national area of priority. The government's response was the 1981 Education Act, which came into force in April 1983. This attempted to legitimate the philosophy of Warnock within a legislative framework. It adopted a relative definition of SEN as 'a learning difficulty which calls for special educational provision to be made' (Education Act 1981: 1.1). This necessitated two further definitions. First, a 'learning difficulty' which was defined as occurring when a child 'has a significantly greater difficulty in learning than the majority of children of his age' or 'has a disability which either prevents or hinders him from making use of educational facilities of a kind generally provided in schools within the area of the local authority concerned, for children of his age' (1981: 1.2). Second, 'special educational provision' which was described as provision different from provision generally made available to children of the same age. In spite of the ambiguous nature of these definitions they have remained virtually unchanged. Early years practitioners are required to use the definitions in the *Code of Practice* (DfES 2001a: 1.3) shown below.

Definition of Special Educational Needs

Children have special educational needs if they have a *learning difficulty* which calls for *special educational provision* to be made for them.

Children have a *learning difficulty* if they:

a) have a significantly greater difficulty in learning than the majority of children the same age; or
b) have a disability which prevents of hinders them from making use of educational facilities of a kind generally provided for children of the same age in schools within the area of the local education authority;
c) are under compulsory school age and fall within the definition at a) or b) above or would do so if special educational provision was not made for them.

Children must not be regarded as having a learning difficulty solely because the language or form of language of their home is different from the language in which they will be taught.

Special educational provision means:

a) for children of 2 or over, educational provision which is additional, or otherwise different from, the educational provision made generally for children of their age in schools maintained by the LEA, other than special schools in the area;

b) for children under 2, educational provision of any kind.

For children under 2 this includes support and advice to help parents help their children.

The lack of clarity and relativity of these official definitions inevitably leads to confusion, causing difficulties in early years policy and practice relating to early identification and assessment of SEN. Whether a child is considered to have a special educational need can vary considerably from area to area, setting to setting and even room to room within the same early education setting. Much depends on the facilities already generally available and the perceived level of difficulty of one child as compared to another. The situation is compounded as a child may not only fall in the SEN category but may also be 'disabled' within the definitions contained in the Children Act 1989 and the Disability Discrimination Act 1995.

Definitions in the Children Act 1989 and the Disability Discrimination Act 1995 are:

A child is disabled if he is blind, deaf or dumb or suffers from a mental disorder of any kind or is substantially and permanently handicapped by illness, injury or congenital deformity or such other disability as may be prescribed.

(Children Act 1989. 17.11)

A person has a disability for the purposes of this Act if he has a physical or mental impairment which has a substantial and long term adverse effect on his ability to carry out normal day-to-day activities.

(Disability Discrimination Act 1995: 1.1)

Models of SEN and disability

There has been a long-standing debate between two distinct models of SEN. First, the *individualistic model*, which attributes learning, physical and sensory difficulties to the individual child. This is often referred to as the 'within child' model and assumes that problems stem from the child's difficulties (Barton and Tomlinson 1981; Tomlinson 1982). It is normally expressed in terms of categories and based on a deficit model. The focus of attention is on the individual learner or child who is deficient in some way or who has the 'problem'. It can also refer to the dominance of medical professionals in 'diagnosis' of a difficulty. Children's needs are described in terms of labels, often synonymous with medical conditions. Mason (1992: 223) offers a succinct definition of this model:

> a medical problem, belonging to the individual concerned, which needs treating, curing or at least ameliorating. It is fundamental to the philosophy of segregation which separates young children from each other on the basis of their medical diagnoses, and then designs a curriculum which is aimed at 'normalising' the child as far as possible.

As these quotes from interviews with early years professionals show (Jones 2000), many practitioners subscribe to this model and see SEN as the child's problem:

> Well, as soon as we realise that *the children have obviously got problems* which will be over and above the average children...
>
> (Nursery teacher)

> Usually by Christmas you can see those that aren't picking things up and you realise that *they have got a problem*.
>
> (Reception teacher)

> You know from the child's last teacher that *a child may or may not have problems*.
>
> (Year 1 teacher)

However, these views do not acknowledge any factors external to the child as contributing to the child's learning difficulty. During the 1980s and early 1990s the limitations of a framework which categorized children according to deficits were recognized. There seemed a significant shift away from attributing difficulties solely to 'within child' factors. The relative concept of 'need' appeared to acknowledge the interactive nature of difficulties. In contrast to the individualistic model, alternative social models were proposed. These models view special needs as socially produced, rather than independent from external factors. In other words, the early education setting, or school system, may be partly responsible (Fulcher 1989; Oliver 1990; Abberley 1992). This viewpoint locates the problem in the interaction between learners and those who work with them, or learning environments, giving rise to outcomes such as inappropriate teaching approaches or hostile attitudes (Oliver 1990). This stance has been criticized as an attempt to deny the reality of disability in that the apparent wish to avoid creating negative labelling effects is tantamount to denying all differences. Non-labelling approaches suggest that 'disability is no problem, it should be disregarded and not seen' (Soder 1992: 254).

One the one hand, we are encouraged to work towards 'inclusion'; on the other, the language of SEN, rooted in the medical model of disability, legitimizes the idea that some children are 'normal' while others are 'special'. As a consequence, groups and individual children are assigned specific labels, often leading to special or segregated provision. This contradicts the notion of inclusion and the drive to make early years settings more inclusive. Early years practitioners need to acknowledge the conflict between the two models and recognize that SEN can be a result of a complex combination of internal and external factors. In addition, staff need to look at common needs rather than focus on the special requirements of particular children. The questions below provide a starting point for discussion:

- What do the practitioners in your setting understand by the term SEN?
- Which children are perceived as having SEN and why?
- Which type of model is dominant in your setting?
- What type of language is used when talking or writing about children with SEN?
- Do you use formal and/or informal labels when talking or writing about children with SEN?

From integration to inclusion

Although the idea of educating children with disabilities alongside their able-bodied friends is not new (Heward and Lloyd-Smith 1990), the Warnock Report (DES 1978) asserted that wherever possible, children with SEN should be educated with their peers. Subsequently, the 1981 Education Act introduced a general duty on LEAs to place as many children as possible who had been receiving education in special schools into ordinary schools. At first sight, the 1981 Act seemed to pave the way for integration of preschool children with SEN into ordinary nursery schools and classes. However, this did not happen on a wide scale, as integration was subject to certain conditions, leaving enormous discretion in the hands of the LEAs. More recently, the government pledged to support the idea of enrolling all children in their local schools using the strongest official line to date: 'unless there are compelling reasons for doing otherwise' (DfEE 1997a: 44). It also suggested that children with SEN should 'join fully with their peers in the curriculum and life of the school'. The original *Code of Practice* (DfE 1994: 1.2) recommended that 'the needs of most pupils will be met in the mainstream ... children with special educational needs ... should, where, appropriate and taking into account the wishes of their parents, be educated alongside their peers in mainstream schools'. The revised *Code* (DfES 2001a: 1.5) re-embraces the fundamental principle that 'the special educational needs of children will normally be met in mainstream schools or settings'. These trends – away from separate and isolated provision for those deemed handicapped, towards special arrangements within services open to all – are encapsulated in the terms 'integration' and more recently 'inclusion'. What do these terms mean and what are their implications for early years settings?

Integration is a common term, yet it covers a wide range of meanings. The word 'integrate' implies putting someone in where they were originally excluded. Simple definitions relate to bringing children from special into mainstream settings, and are concerned with the placement of individual children rather than the narrowing of social and educational gaps between them. Attitudes toward integration vary from those who pledge support for the integration of all children experiencing difficulties or with disabilities, to those who are in favour of retaining segregated provision. However, integration and segregation are not mutually exclusive and may exist even within a single setting (Hegarty 1993; Sinclair-Taylor 1995). There is no guarantee that the placement of children with disabilities in an early education setting, for example, automatically results in integrating activities. More complex interpretations view integration as a process rather than a state, a process of planned and continuous interaction with other children within common educational systems and settings. Slee (1993) questions whether integration is understood as an outsider coming in, or as creating a culture so that schools or educational settings accept all comers. From this viewpoint, integration is seen as a proper concern for all young children rather than an initiative focused on SEN. It is not simply a question of responding to disability but of extending education and social justice to all young children. The terms 'integration' and 'inclusion' appear to be related but different, in that inclusion refers not only to placement, but also to the quality of that placement. However, is inclusion simply a new term for old ideas or is it an entirely different concept to integration?

The process of inclusion

Whether the focus is within education or beyond, inclusion in early childhood implies change that is different from that suggested by the term integration. Inclusion is not a fixed state but a flexible and moving process: 'Inclusive education is not integration and is not concerned with the accommodation and assimilation of discriminated groups' (Barton 1999: 58). First, inclusion is regarded as an attitude or principle, a means of promoting an ethos which redefines 'normality' as accepting and valuing diversity. Second, inclusion is viewed as an end product, a non-segregated system of early years education. Third, the term draws attention to the quality of mainstream settings for children with and without SEN. Fourth, a more recent and radical standpoint views inclusion as not only relating to education, but to society at large. The intentions and values are part of a vision of an inclusive society of which education is a part (Barton 1999).

Responding to difference

Inclusion suggests an ethos of respect for individuals within a common educational framework. It acknowledges some differential treatment, since clearly children are all different. However, the inclusive response is to celebrate and appreciate those differences rather than categorize, label and segregate. An inclusive education system regards diversity as ordinary. Inclusion is concerned with the coming together of communities and attitudes towards diversity and differences within social groups (Forest and Pearpoint 1992). It is about recognizing and valuing individuals, without making any one child, or group of children, feel less valued than the rest. Supporters of inclusive educational settings describe a place where children learn together, where parents will want their children to have friendships with the other members of the group regardless of individual difference. In this context, the idea of identifying learning needs and devising, implementing and monitoring appropriate programmes is applicable for all children. It leads to a situation where every child is special 'but none so extraordinary as to merit exclusion' (Hegarty 1993: 67).

It has to be acknowledged that the rhetoric of total inclusion is problematic. A single system to include all children and all resources, staff, expertise and learning materials from special and mainstream education presupposes that all early years practitioners would welcome all children, including the severely mentally handicapped, autistic and blind. It also ignores parental choice and educational priorities, such as the attainment of self-help skills (Lewis 1995). The assumption is that all parents would, given a choice, opt for mainstream early education settings.

Philosophically, there may appear to be no obstacle preventing the placement of any child with SEN or disabilities, whatever their complexity, at least in terms of education, in a mainstream early education setting. Many practitioners would agree with the fundamental principle of the inclusive school or setting – in other words, all children should learn together regardless of any difficulties or differences they may have. However, change on this scale involves a political will and major professional development in attitudes towards difference, in pedagogy and in curriculum organization. It requires financial backing for resources and staff training and support, together with willingness and competence from early childhood educators. In some cases, inclusion may require a long-term radical overhaul of what early education settings have to offer.

Booth *et al.* (1997) also remind us that the notion of inclusion cannot refer to some children and not others. They suggest that inclusion requires the removal of barriers to learning for *all* children. In this sense, it is not relevant to ask whether a child with a disability can join mainstream education settings, but how the circumstances in early years provision can be arranged in a way that makes the educational development of each child possible. If inclusion were viewed as 'a value to be followed' rather than 'an experiment to be tested' (Ferguson and Asch 1989 cited in Ballard 1999: 2), then concerns about inclusion would go beyond disability to encompass all young children. Rather than focus on labelling and making decisions regarding placements, the emphasis shifts to adapting the curriculum and providing support based on the individual requirements of all children. Armstrong (1999: 76) develops this point, offering a definition of inclusive education that moves the debate well beyond concerns regarding children with SEN: 'a system of education which recognises the right of all children and young people to share a common educational environment in which all are valued equally, regardless of differences in perceived ability, gender, class, ethnicity or learning styles'.

It is from this standpoint that we need to work towards creating an early years setting with an inclusive culture that accepts diversity as normal and includes all children within a common educational framework. *Birth to Three Matters* (Sure Start 2003) supports this idea for babies and toddlers, stating that 'Although their responses may differ, children with disabilities or learning difficulties are entitled to the same range of experiences as others'.

Effective education for all

Few early years workers would dispute that all children have a right to an effective early years education and a number of writers have made links between the processes involved in developing inclusive schools and the characteristics of effective schooling (Fulcher 1989; Ainscow 1991; Slee 1993). Ainscow (1991) suggests that rather than attempting to define special children and creating special methods of teaching them, we should focus attention on developing effective teaching and learning for all. This encompasses the idea that attempts to improve teaching and learning strategies for all children may well be the best way forward in meeting the needs of those hitherto described as having SEN. It has been argued that inclusion must not be regarded as a technical problem related to measures such as resources rather than fundamental attitudes. Early educational settings are not simply buildings or curriculum plans. More importantly, they are relationships and interactions between people. The *Code of Practice* (DfES 2001a) reflects this broader stance and includes as a critical success factor that 'the culture, management and deployment of resources in a school or setting are designed to ensure *all children's needs are met*' (1.5, original emphasis).

Making exclusion visible

Developing inclusion in early childhood involves two complementary processes: first, the process of increasing participation of children and second, the process of decreasing exclusionary pressures (Booth *et al.* 1997; Booth and Ainscow 2002). Pressures to exclude spring from a variety of sources including fear, ignorance and prejudice, negative labelling, stereotyping and stigmatizing. Inclusion demands changes in values, priorities and policies that support exclusion (Barton 1999). A high priority for early years practitioners is to promote inclusion by making exclusion visible in their settings. The reasons why exclusive practices continue to be observed in early years settings can be divided into four broad groups. First, there are physical barriers such as unsuitable and inaccessible buildings and facilities, cluttered furniture and hard floors, toilet facilities outside main playrooms, lack of nappy-changing facilities, inaccessible resources, unsuitable storage and unsuitable outdoor play space. It is important to examine your learning environment and look for ways to improve access. Unfortunately, physical barriers are often used as an 'excuse' for not admitting children with disabilities.

While physical barriers can be improved it is far more challenging to break down the second category of resistance to inclusion: the attitude or view that some children can never be fully included. This is highlighted by the continued use of negative labelling, the language of SEN and the dominance of the 'medical' model of disability. Children may be selected for admission provided no adaptations or extra support are needed to accommodate their needs. However, ignorance, prejudice and stereotypical attitudes towards certain groups of children perceived as 'different' prevail.

A third obstacle is the political nature of educational provision. This includes the confusing nature of official definitions and the distinction between disability and SEN, and the continued investment in and existence of separate preschool and nursery groups segregating some young children from others (notably children with sensory impairments, learning difficulties or difficult behaviour). The rationale for the maintenance of a separate system is rooted in the perception that special education is beneficial for individual children. This idea that separating children is somehow in their best interests is somewhat at odds with the current rhetoric of inclusion.

Fourth, in the maintained, private and voluntary sectors, limited financial resources to improve facilities or employ extra staff can inhibit the process of inclusion. The low professional status and lack of training for *all staff* on inclusion awareness, plus a lack of trained or qualified learning support assistants available in early education settings provided for children of preschool age, aggravate the situation.

Working towards inclusive practice

Booth and Ainscow (2002) identify three dimensions in the promotion of inclusion. In relation to the early years these are: creating inclusive cultures in early years settings; developing inclusive practice in the early years; and producing inclusive early years policies. They offer a number of indicators and questions to help practitioners plan and review practice in each of these dimensions. The first two have been developed and adapted below to apply specifically to early years settings. The policy dimension is developed later on in this book.

Creating inclusive cultures

This dimension is concerned with building community and establishing inclusive values. The early years setting plays an important role in its community, as it is often the first point of contact between home and group education or childcare. Everyone should be made to feel welcome. Parents and members of the local community should have opportunities to be fully involved and contribute to the setting's activities. Staff need to establish inclusive values in which there are high expectations for all children. All staff should share a philosophy for inclusion and children are equally valued regardless of their differences. Relationships between adults and adults, and children and children are positive and discrimination is minimized. However, as the case study below shows, individual experiences still fall short of these ideals.

Case example

Tom is a 4-year-old boy who was diagnosed as autistic when he was 18 months' old. He attended a mainstream private nursery. When he was almost 4 the educational psychologist suggested the possibility of attending a mainstream school, with full-time support. Tom's parents went to look at their local village primary school. They encountered unexpected hostility. The headteacher made it clear that Tom would be regarded as a burden to the school resources. Even though Tom's mother had explained that Tom would have an assistant to support him, both Tom and the 'extra adult' were regarded as a potential problem which the school could do without. Tom's mum recalls what happened:

Yeah, because Mr Smith, he said to me that there's not the space in the school. There's not the time and he was quite honest, but he was quite [mother was crying at this point], well I nearly punched his head in. He as good as said no, I don't need another special needs kid in this school. He more or less said another adult in the classroom – the size of these classrooms. He just said you know the teachers we've got haven't got time to go round now without having my boy. So he was quite honest about it, but the way he spoke to me, he was really hard and it quite upset me.

Tom's mother was clearly given the impression that this headteacher was making an excuse not to accept Tom into the school. He appeared to make no secret of the fact that the school was unwilling to include Tom. By contrast, Merfield was a smaller school in the next village. Spaces were available as the school was in a less popular geographical position. Tom's mother described how she felt when Tom was offered a place in the reception class:

> *I think Mr Willis made us feel at ease straight away. He was willing to help and he was willing to give him a chance, that was the main thing. And he looked at Tom as a person before his disability and he still does now.*

In terms of creating inclusive cultures it is essential for all early years workers to reflect on how people feel when they visit or join the group and on the impression given to parents, visitors and children. The questions below could be discussed and used as a basis for moving your setting towards a more inclusive approach.

Questions for your reflection

1 Is the first contact people have with the setting friendly and welcoming?
2 Does the setting provide opportunities for welcoming parents and members of the local community in, to participate in activities?
3 Are all children welcome regardless of difference?
4 Is information available in other forms of language?
5 Does the information for new parents make it clear that the setting is one which routinely welcomes and responds to the full range of children?
6 Do staff and parents feel a sense of 'ownership' and 'belonging' to the group?
7 Do displays and entrance areas reflect the local community?
8 Do displays represent collaborative as well as individual achievements?
9 Are children encouraged to help each other share and be friendly with all other children?
10 Is there a strong partnership between staff and parents/carers?
11 Are attitudes about the limits of inclusion challenged, such as in the case of children with severe impairments?
12 Is there a shared wish to accept all children in the local community?
13 Is diversity viewed as a positive resource for learning rather than a problem?
14 Do children feel that adults 'like' them?
15 Do staff avoid labelling children in relation to their ability?

Developing inclusive practice

This dimension relates to teaching and learning. In an inclusive early childhood environment, activities are planned with the needs of all children in mind. They involve active participation and collaboration. The atmosphere is one of respect and activities and resources promote positive images. Assessment helps all children progress. Resources in the setting and in the community are used to support learning and partici-pation. Staff expertise should be used and outside support agencies known and used.

Questions for your reflection

1   Are activities planned to support the children's learning rather than deliver the curriculum?
2   Is there a suitable variety of activities and are they adapted to maxi-mize participation?
3   Do activities focus on personal, social and emotional as well as cog-nitive achievements?
4   Do activities encourage children to play cooperatively and commu-nicate with adults and children?
5   Are additional adults used to improve the learning of all children?
6   Are children given opportunities to take responsibility for their own learning?
7   Are children's own experiences used to develop activities?
8   Are children given opportunities to represent their achievements in a variety of ways?
9   Is planning a shared activity making full use of all adults?
10 Are resources used to support learning and participation?
                    (Adapted from Booth and Ainscow 2002: 41–53, 71–85)

Conclusion

Working towards inclusive early years education will take time. Inclu-sion in early childhood involves valuing all children and staff equally. It demands increasing participation and reducing exclusion from the cul-ture, curricula and communities of local early education provision. It calls for a restructuring of the policies and practices of early education settings in order to respond to the diverse needs of all children in the local area. Inclusion is concerned with reducing barriers to learning for all children, not just those perceived as having SEN or an impairment, and acknowledging explicitly the right of all children to an education in their locality (Booth and Ainscow 2002). Changing policies, attitudes and practices is a demanding task. However, as a leaflet entitled *'Ten Reasons for Inclusion'* produced by the Centre for Studies on Inclusive Education suggests, it is important to remember 'Inclusive education is a human right, it's good education, and it makes good social sense'.

● ● ●

2

Early identification and assessment

The importance of early identification, assessment and provision for any child who may have special educational needs cannot be over-emphasised.

(DfE 1994: 1.3)

This chapter highlights the dilemmas facing practitioners when deciding whether or not to identify young children as having SEN. It uses quotes from early years practitioners in a study by Jones (2000) to illustrate the problematic and complex nature, purposes and consequences of early identification and assessment. It provides a general overview of the common forms and purposes of educational assessment, including formative, summative and baseline assessment. The theme is extended in the next chapter, which focuses on the graduated assessment model recommended in the *Code of Practice* (DfES 2001a), which will form the basis of your SEN policy and procedures for identifying and providing for children with perceived SEN.

All schools and early education settings, including childminder networks, are required by law to identify, assess and provide for children with SEN. A constant theme in the education of young children with SEN is that of early identification. Historically, the purpose of early identification is associated with the need to identify and place those who are considered to be somehow deviant in relation to a 'norm'. Intelligence test results, for example, were often used to create formal social labels for groups of children, who were categorized as 'bright' or 'dull'.

As a result of the assessment and labelling process a whole range of categories were used to describe varying degrees of 'difference'. The following passage suggests that the notion of early identification was originally based on a need to recognize a potentially troublesome section of the population:

> The feeble-minded are a parasitic, predatory class, never capable of self-support or of managing their own affairs ... they cause unutterable sorrow at home and are a menace and danger to the community. Feeble minded women are almost invariably immoral, and if at large usually become carriers of venereal disease or give birth to children who are as defective as themselves ... every feeble minded person, especially the high grade imbecile, is a potential criminal ... the unrecognised imbecile is a most dangerous element in the community.
>
> (Fernald 1912, cited in Armstrong 1996: 2)

By contrast, the position today is that early identification and assessment is desirable and will benefit children in the longer term. This is known as the *compensatory view*. The argument is simple and superficially persuasive: in order to help children with SEN we should identify their difficulties as soon as possible. By so doing we can then provide interventions which will remedy the problem or prevent it from becoming more serious.

The original *Code of Practice* stressed the significance of identifying children with perceived SEN at the earliest possible moment, stating that 'The importance of early identification, assessment and provision for any child who may have special educational needs cannot be over-emphasised' (DfE 1994: 1.3). This was reiterated in the current version which includes as a critical success factor that 'LEAs, schools and settings should work together to ensure that any child's special educational needs are *identified early*' ((DfES 2001a: 1.6, original emphasis).

The Green Paper (DfEE 1997a: 1.5) also suggests that the 'best way to tackle educational disadvantage is to get in early'. Using the language of the medical model it recommends 'early diagnosis' in order to improve children's prospects later on. This in turn has financial implications and early identification is regarded as a way of reducing 'expensive intervention' later in the child's education. Early identification and assessment is viewed as a means of 'doing good', a process carried out purely for the benefit of the child. In the study carried out by Jones (2000) all respondents in the case study schools stressed the desire to identify the children's needs as soon as possible and had faith in the positive outcomes of early action. A headteacher suggested, 'Early identification is essential. It is absolutely essential'. The nursery teacher agreed: 'We must catch these children early. I think it's essential to concentrate on the nursery end of the school. Definitely'. There was an overwhelming consensus that early identification and intervention was an effective means of avoiding more serious difficulties later on. The use of the word 'catch', repeated more than once, conveys the idea that 'these children' should be 'caught' or separated in some way from the rest of the group. The original *Code* also suggests that 'the earlier action is taken, the more responsive a child is likely to be' (DfE 1994: 2.16). A nursery nurse who had supported special needs groups for eight years did not need convincing:

> I think it's essential. I think if you don't catch it while it's young and sort it out it becomes a bigger problem later and I think all the help that can be given should be given when they're tiny. As young as you can, catch 'em so that you can eradicate most of the problems before they become bigger ones. They've got to get their skills up to the skills of their peers.

In the wider context, a head of learning support services expressed a similar philosophy: 'The support staff here want to do it, because by the time they've got a kid, the difficulties are so entrenched that they've got years of work ahead. And they all think that if they could have worked earlier they could have solved a lot'.

A school SENCO also expressed concern at the possibility of children's difficulties becoming more pronounced as they moved up through the school: 'The pity of it is if, if you could get into the infants now while the gap isn't so wide and perhaps bring them back up to the level of the majority of the class'.

The Green Paper suggests, 'When educational failure becomes entrenched, pupils can move from demoralisation to disruptive behaviour and truancy' (DfEE 1997a: 1.5). However, if failure becomes 'entrenched' at an early age then logically, early intervention could have an adverse rather than a positive effect. This headteacher observed that characteristics evident at the age of 4 or 5 were still present later on, in a variety of aspects: 'the children who have the tantrums in reception are more likely to be those who have difficulty later on. Those who are well motivated and well adjusted in reception are unlikely to change later on.'

Identifying and assessing children's needs is time-consuming, complex and depends partly on your philosophy on early identification and partly on the mechanisms available for assessment. While there are obviously some benefits to early identification, some teachers in the study (Jones 2000) expressed reservations regarding premature labelling and maturity issues. A teacher with 20 years' experience in reception acknowledged that experiences before starting school can influence a child's progress and recognized the inherent danger in labelling a child as 'special' too soon:

> I find it very, very difficult in reception, especially the ones who haven't been to nursery. I don't like to jump in straight away and say this child's got special needs. I've got one little girl and I thought at first, oh my goodness, we're never going to get anywhere. But she's really come on. She used to go out for support but she doesn't even do that now and she's coping.

This reception teacher had already formed a premature assumption about this child which she later had to question. The little girl had obviously made considerable progress in her first term at school. The use of the word 'coping' suggests that this may have been a case of a child who took time to adjust to the reception class environment. The question remains as to how a child can be judged to be 'coping'. Does 'coping' equate with 'learning'? Another reception teacher at another school agreed that maturity was an issue:

> There is also the maturity problem. Some children are much less mature than others. My green grapes, the younger ones, they came in scribbling and now they can copy or write their names or attempt to, it's like a child who has been to nursery, they'll score high, but the others will catch up.

Much depends on the needs of the child and in some cases intervention may be more appropriate at a later stage when a child is more mature (Lindsay and Desforges 1998). The difficulties posed by the complex notion of early identification were expressed by another head-teacher in the study by Jones (2000). She noted the dilemma of deciding when children's needs were within the 'normal' range and when needs were significant enough to warrant further concern. Children were notionally divided into two groups: first, those with 'obvious' difficulties and second, those who were in a sort of twilight zone who may be 'underachieving' or may 'catch up'. The headteacher attempts to explain the dilemma:

> Well, generally speaking we want to support mainstream children within the class, which may be just underachievement because at reception age it's very difficult to define which children are underachieving and which are special needs ... it's very difficult to tell as they may well be very different. We keep a weather eye on all

the children and the children we're talking about, they do stand out as significantly underachieving for a variety of reasons. But again we do use the PIPS [local baseline] information... to to help us decide. But the children who are working at the lower end of the class we still watch.

However, while most practitioners would agree with the idea of early identification, others would advise caution: 'the first thing is not to jump to conclusions ... there is no point in intervening, perhaps inappropriately, before there is some clarity about what is needed' (Roffey 1999: 53).

Assessment as a lifelong process

Assessment is a lifelong process. It can take many forms and lead to a variety of positive or negative consequences. Severe and complex disabilities are often, but not always, noticed at or shortly after birth and in some cases even before birth. Where a child is causing concern, they would be regularly assessed by the health service. Health visitors carry out home visits to ascertain the levels of support required. All children under 5 are routinely screened to identify any concerns – for example, through a check-up at 6 weeks old and follow-up hearing tests and developmental checks. A child under 5 suspected of having learning or developmental difficulties or delays may be referred by the health visitor to local support services – for example, speech therapists or home visitors – with parental permission. However, if the child needs to be seen by a medical practitioner this must be via the general practitioner (GP) where continued assessment by medical professionals, usually the hospital paediatrician at a Child Development Centre (CDC), would take place.

At death friends and family assess our achievements in life and in between birth and death we are constantly assessed in one way or another, no more so than as children in the education system. Since the introduction of the National Curriculum and its associated national statutory assessment procedures, primary school children have come into the realm of tests and assessment methods formerly reserved for older pupils. Gipps and Stobart (1993: 1) observed that 'Pupils currently going through compulsory education in England and Wales will be among the most assessed the state education system has ever produced'. At the time of this observation, the first statutory assessment was at the end of Key Stage 1. However, the Education Act 1997 introduced compulsory baseline assessment of children within weeks of entry to school, implemented from September 1998. Although replaced in 2003 by the *Foundation Stage Profile* (DfES 2003) these measures have encompassed a whole new and very young cohort of children into the assessment system.

Baseline assessment

Although statutory baseline assessment has now been replaced by the foundation stage profile, it is likely that LEAs will use some sort of 'one off' baseline as a way of allocating SEN resources to schools, as was the case before statutory baseline assessment was introduced. Baseline assessment appeared to serve a dual role in enabling children to be assessed in order to assist the future planning of their education and to provide a means of measuring their future educational achievement.

Lindsay (1998) groups the purposes of baseline assessment into two key categories: first, those which focus on the child, including early identification of children with SEN, early identification of children's specific difficulties and the continuous monitoring of all children's progress; second, those which focus on whole-school issues such as planning resources, school improvement and measuring the effectiveness of teaching. Wolfendale (1993) summarizes a number of concerns about baseline assessment. She suggests, for example, that it may lead to a narrowing of the curriculum and she questions the impact of early labelling on teacher expectations. If children are grouped according to the results of initial assessments, this could lead to a cycle of low expectation becoming a self-fulfilling prophesy.

Lindsay and Desforges (1998) argue that there are inherent conflicts in using baseline assessment for identifying children's learning needs as well as treating it as a starting point for plotting future educational achievement in order to determine the relative value added by the school. Apart from questions regarding the technical quality of the schemes, they question whether one instrument can actually fulfil such a variety of purposes. Lindsay (2000) provides a useful and up to date review of baseline assessment with particular reference to SEN. His analysis suggests that national baseline assessment is not especially helpful to children perceived as having SEN. He points out that there are 'dangers as well as positive opportunities in trying to use baseline assessment as a means of identifying children with SEN'. If the results are seen as evidence of 'learning difficulties' he suggests that there is a 'significant likelihood of inappropriate labelling and provision' (Lindsay 2000: 133).

As discussed in the next chapter, the child who scores low on the baseline or the foundation stage profile may be processed through the graduated assessment procedures recommended in the *Code of Practice*, a process which does not necessarily guarantee positive outcomes. As Lindsay and Desforges (1998) point out, users of baseline assessment cannot assume that measures at age 5 can identify children who 'have' SEN. There is no absolute standard to determine whether a child has SEN, particularly in the early years when the normal range of development is wide. Instead they suggest the results may be a useful indication of SEN arising from the interaction between the child and the child's early education environment: family and community.

The foundation stage profile is certainly a more formative process than baseline assessment, which was summative. Assessment takes place throughout reception class rather than at a single point in time and recognizes the contribution of previous practitioners, parents and children to the assessment process. Overtly, the purpose appears to be to help plan for children's learning needs. However, if the numerical scales are used to predict scores in Key Stage 1 tests or as a mechanism for identifying and grouping children by ability, the questions applicable to a national baseline will remain unresolved.

Formative and summative assessment

Undoubtedly, assessment can be viewed as a positive process. Satterly (1989) introduces his book on assessment in schools by tracing the origins of the word 'assessment' to the Latin root *assidere* meaning to sit beside. Conner (1991) extends this by adding the Latin root of educational, *educare* meaning 'to bring out'. Logically, he concludes that educational assessment should mean sitting beside and bringing out the potential that exists within children and providing certain opportunities for them to show what they can do. Viewed in this way assessment becomes a positive and integral feature in improving teaching and learning. It seems that the purpose of assessment is to provide appropriate help for children. The implication is that assessment should be an ongoing and formative process of observing children's progress and planning for their individual needs.

Most commentators agree that the central purpose of educational assessment should be to promote children's learning. The key function of the assessment process is to identify where children are in their learning in order to plan the next steps: 'it can yield a basis for planning the next educational steps in response to children's needs ... it should be an integral part of the educational process ... it needs to be incorporated systematically into teaching strategies and practices at all levels' (TGAT 1988: paras 3–4). The following quote from the foreword of the *Foundation Stage Profile* document (DfES 2003) also recognizes this:

> To help children progress, practitioners need information about what the children know, understand and can do. Through observing children at work, and by making notes when necessary about what has been achieved, practitioners can make professional judgments about their children's achievements and decide on the next steps in learning. They can also provide information for parents and carers on how children are progressing. This process, known as 'assessment for learning', is central to raising achievement ... I hope its sensible and straightforward approach will mark a new era in assessment practice.

The profile suggests the central purposes of assessment of 3- to 5-year-olds are to provide information for practitioners and parents and to raise achievement. This approach is based on the professional ability of those working with young children to be able to make and record assessments on children as and when appropriate to help them move forward in their learning. The method of assessment is through ongoing observations and recording of children's achievements. This is characteristic of formative assessment. Observing children in different situations and participating in different activities over a few weeks will provide a lot of information. Watching interactions with other children, levels of play and communication will give a good idea of what the child can achieve with and without help. Brief entries in a notebook will provide a wealth of information for discussion with parents and colleagues (Roffey 1999).

Intervention based on this type of assessment should make a difference and would seem appropriate for all children, not just those with SEN. While recognizing that there may be a need for alternative forms of assessment for some children, the foundation stage profile has been developed to be inclusive 'so that as many children as possible can be assessed against the scales' (DfES 2003: 113). This has been achieved by providing examples specifically relating to children with individual needs, giving guidance for the assessment of children with a range of needs. Assessments for the profile are based on 'cumulative evidence from practitioner observations of children during ongoing learning and teaching' (DfES 2003: 114). Therefore, assessment is supposed to be a continuous process of collecting and reviewing information in order to help children succeed (Ainscow 1988). However, as the succinct definition below shows, the assessment of children with SEN can also relate specifically to decisions regarding resources and special provision:

> Assessment is a decision making process whereby a child's strengths and weaknesses are evaluated in order to come to a clearer understanding of the nature of his special educational needs, in relation to environmental resources, and the provision which could best meet those needs.
>
> (Goacher *et al.* 1988: 97)

Continuous assessment is commonplace in preschools and nursery classes where there is no statutory assessment. The *Code of Practice* recognizes that a continuous cycle of planning, teaching and assessment is a part of any educational environment. In nurseries and preschool groups, formative assessment includes strategies such as focused and general observation, talking and listening to the children and questioning. In reception and Key Stage 1 classes it could involve marking and feedback, teacher-designed tests and, again, observation and questioning. As the following quotes from Jones (2000) illustrate, teachers tend to assess the nature of children's needs through a combination of strategies, predominantly observation or comparison with peers and often including intuitive 'ad hoc' or 'gut' feelings based on experience: 'Well, really it was just a case of comparing their work to other children's work and instinctive I think as well'. One teacher thought she could identify the children with potential learning difficulties in an unproblematic way: 'Because of course, although there are some children you know who are going to catch up during their time, because they do make enormous progress, there are some that *you just know* are going to need specific support'.

Reception teachers can also use information passed on from the child's previous setting. At Willowbank School in the Midlands, for example, as many as 40 of the 48 children entering the reception classes may have attended the part-time nursery on the school site. In this case, the nursery teacher is a valuable source of information on the children prior to starting school and plays an important role in early identification of children with SEN. A reception teacher explains: 'So we are looking at what they have done beforehand, what they have done in nursery, the observations there. We're looking to see if there are any children who are very different from the normal cohort.'

Again this illustrates the idea of being able to identify children perceived as different from an expected 'norm'. The nursery teacher began the process and had visited the children's homes before they entered nursery. She had devised a written assessment record for every child which was carried out at the beginning of the academic year – in other words, in the September following the child's third birthday: 'We've got a baseline that we do for nursery, which is actually in our assessment booklet. It goes through physical development, cognitive development, fine motor skills, gross motor and their social skills of course' (nursery teacher). This was then added to by the teacher and the nursery nurse, making notes during session times and building up a detailed written profile of each child by the end of the year. This assessment was seen as a valuable information-gathering exercise, in order to help plan any extra input that might be needed at a later date:

> We start of at the lowest point, the cognitive area. For example, we start off with matching colours and if they're not able to do that, we will note it and come back to that once we've filled in the different areas of the assessment booklet, and we've actually seen what they can do. And we will come back to that and organise small group activities often to help them.
>
> (Nursery teacher)

Once the initial assessment had been completed the two nursery staff then consulted, at the end of the first half term, to see if there were any more concerns, as they then knew the children better: 'For instance, at the beginning of the year we felt that John, Simon and Hannah were the children who were delayed in various aspects of their language development'. These 3-year-olds were then marked out for ongoing observation and discussion during the nursery year. By the time they entered school they were already on the school SEN register at one of the stages of assessment in the *Code of Practice*. By contrast, at another school, Merfield, children came from a wide variety of preschool settings including the preschool playgroup in the local church hall and a fee-paying private day nursery. Only 4 of the 24 children in reception attended the LEA nursery, which was five miles away on another primary school site. Initially, therefore, Merfield relied on parental information and the LEA baseline data:

> In terms of a baseline we send out a questionnaire to the parents. The parents actually let us know the sort of things they can do, fine motor things and so on, whether they can tie their shoelace, you know, whether they can get dressed and this sort of thing; what the children enjoy doing, if they are beginning to read, whatever, whatever the parent wants to put on.
>
> (Headteacher, Merfield)

Whatever methods of gathering information are used, early years practitioners should be concerned with how the processes of assessment can assist children's learning. Assessment is not a distinct activity but can be a natural part of teaching and learning routines. It should be a 'built in' rather than a 'bolted on' part of the curriculum. The following steps in the formative assessment process illustrate the point:

- identify the learning objective for various activities at the stepping stone level – for example, counting to ten and beyond;
- note the opportunities the child will have to demonstrate successfully achieving the objective – for example, jumping on trampoline and counting jumps, counting bricks in a tower, counting children at register;
- observe how far the child counts correctly, on a number of occasions;
- talk to the child about what he/she has done;
- record anything significant – for example, if the child counted to 19;
- modify teaching plan or target for the child, to manage next stage of learning.

When children have grasped something and they are using it in their play situations you know they have achieved it. Assessment in early childhood should focus on positive achievement. Instead of asking 'what can't this child do' in relation to children with additional needs, we should ask 'what we can do in order to help this child make progress?' In this way we can embrace every child within a common assessment framework.

Summative assessment

Where formative assessment is an ongoing process, summative assessment normally takes place at a certain point in time. It is a 'one off' activity designed to provide information about a child's attainment or performance as compared with other children. Its function is primarily one of gaining information to share with others. A central feature of the 1988 Education Reform Act was the setting up of the National Curriculum and an associated framework of statutory assessment. This marked a watershed in the history of assessment as the focus shifted from formative teacher assessments to a national system of summative tests at the end of each of the National Curriculum key stages. Lewis (1996) examines what has been learned about the use of summative assessment of primary-aged children perceived as having SEN. She concludes that the statutory arrangements are devised for national monitoring purposes and not to assist in the planning of any individual's learning. This change of focus underpinned another major function of assessment which

Lindsay and Desforges (1998) term 'evaluative'. Here, assessment takes place in order to provide evidence for public consumption. The results are linked to the notion of accountability. As Gipps and Stobart (1993: 98) state: 'The aggregated summative information is there for accountability and political purposes; it is there to evaluate and monitor schools rather than to help directly in the education of individual children'.

Conclusion

While formative, summative and baseline assessments have inevitable implications for children with SEN, both the original and revised *Code of Practice* establish a completely separate model specifically designed to identify and assess this group of children. The purposes and consequences of using this separate graduated model in early years settings are discussed in the next chapter.

3

A *graduated model of assessment and provision*

The crux of the problem is the IEPs. How are they to be
formulated, what time is available to formulate them and
subjective assessment of their worth.

(Lewis et al. 1996: 38)

The assessment process is the most crucial aspect of special education. It
is 'literally the point at which certain children are judged to be different
from others' (Tomlinson 1982: 82). This chapter provides an overview of
the graduated model of assessment specifically recommended and
designed for children with SEN. This model forms the total process of
determining which children require and receive special educational
provision. The chapter begins by making the distinction between
assessment as a continuous feature of teaching and learning for all
children and assessment as a professional decision-making process
associated with the provision of resources for particular children. It then
moves on to explain the practical implications of the graduated model of
assessment recommended in the *Code of Practice* (DfES 2001a), specifically
focusing on the content and characteristics of the stages of assessment
referred to as '*Early Years Action*' and '*Early Years Action Plus*' and
explains the formulation of individual education plans (IEPs) as a central
feature of the graduated approach. The chapter provides an overview of
the final stages of the assessment procedure where the LEA takes lead
responsibility for making decisions regarding special educational provision for individual children and concludes that the graduated model
may appear inclusive but can also be exclusive.

Assessment as a decision-making process

According to the Warnock Report (DES 1978) the education service is in an ideal position to identify signs of special need, especially in nursery schools or classes, and this is one of the advantages of nursery education. Nevertheless, the assessment procedure is complex. It has to reconcile the interests and needs of all those concerned: the child, the parents, the LEA and practitioners. Sometimes these interests may be conflicting. The Warnock Report claims that, in order to be effective, assessment should involve parents, look at the aspect which is causing concern, discover how a child learns over a period of time and take into account family and school circumstances (DES 1978: 4.29–33). Assessments may also be influenced by contextual factors and professional value positions. In their research on the assessment procedures introduced by the 1981 Act, Goacher *et al.* (1988) point out the distinction between assessment which is a continuous feature of attempts to help children with difficulties, and statutory assessment which takes place in order for an LEA to determine the provision which should be made in a particular case where the setting or school resources alone are not sufficient to meet a child's needs, suggesting that the assessment of children with SEN relates specifically to decisions regarding resources and special provision: 'Assessment is a decision making process whereby a child's strengths and weaknesses are evaluated in order to come to a clearer understanding of the nature of his special educational needs, in relation to environmental resources, and the provision which could best meet those needs' (Goacher *et al.* 1988: 97).

It is important for practitioners to recognize the distinction between assessment as a 'professional' decision concerned with meeting a child's needs, and assessment as an 'administrative' process relating to the allocation of resources (Welton *et al.* 1982). It is the 'professionals' who have the control at both levels. Chasty and Friel (1991: 31) summarize the link between ongoing monitoring and decisions regarding provision, commenting that:

> The purpose of the assessment process must be to survey all the influences on a child's learning, so enabling a teaching programme to be implemented which meets the child's needs. The wider and more 'in depth' this process is, the more likely it is to convey an accurate picture of the range of abilities and difficulties apparent in the child's learning, and the more appropriate the provision will be.

Withers and Lee (1988), in a discussion of assessment as ideology, contend that educational assessment is the exercise of power and at the same time a natural extension of the everyday judgements which any professional makes about the children in their care. They point out that although the process of selection is overtly 'scientific, neutral and benevolent', assessment can be a highly divisive and political process of selection for special schooling albeit within the mainstream or in a separate school or unit:

> A process which alters the future treatment and life chances of children, and which is sometimes the means by which pupils are selected for special provision ... the separation of a group of troublesome pupils from the mainstream, the preservation of a clientele for a group of professionals, the satisfaction of a need of professionals to be seen as coping in their teaching in the mainstream and so on.
>
> (Withers and Lee 1988: 175, 181)

The graduated model of assessment

The idea of a staged assessment procedure originated in the Warnock Report (DES 1978), which envisaged five stages of assessment ranging from teacher assessment to multidisciplinary assessment by specialists. The *Code of Practice* (DfE 1994) adopted this model with an IEP at each stage from initial concern to a statement of SEN. The revised *Code* collapsed these five stages into two. However, as Table 3.1 illustrates, beneath the administrative surface the five stages remain intact. The *Code* involves all those working with young children and attempts to link assessment more directly with decisions about the curriculum and provision. It is expected that the process should take place whether or not the child has reached statutory school age. It is up to the individual setting to decide the exact procedures adopted, but 'Early education settings should adopt graduated response so as to be able to provide specific help to individual young children' (DfES 2001a: 4:10). Although it is commonly accepted that children progress at different rates, the trigger for action is evidence that the child is not making 'adequate' progress. The *Code* (DfES 2001a: 4:14) defines 'adequate progress' as progress that achieves one or more of the following:

- closes the attainment gap between the child and the majority of children in the same age group;
- prevents the attainment gap growing wider;
- attainment is similar to that of other children starting from the same baseline as the majority of peers;
- matches or improves upon the child's previous rate of progress;

Table 3.1 The five stages of assessment portrayed from 1978–2001

Warnock's five stages (1978)	Code of Practice (1994)	Code of Practice (2001)
Stage 1: class teacher/ headteacher collect information and make arrangements for in-school support. Inform parents. Monitor and review.	Stage 1: class teacher or early years worker express and record initial concerns, gather information and make arrangements for differentiation. Inform parents. Monitor and review.	Early Years Action. Information gathering, IEP in place for child recoding additional provision and strategies. Special educational needs coordinator (SENCO) and staff monitor and review.
Stage 2: class teacher discusses difficulty with special education expert teacher. Provide specialist programme.	Stage 2: IED, target setting. Discuss with SENCO. Monitor and review.	
Stage 3: assessment by external agency (e.g. GP or educational psychologist) (three school-based stages).	Stage 3: seek advice from external agencies.	Early Years Action Plus. Involvement of outside agencies.
Stage 4: multi-professional assessment.	Stage 4: LEA multidisciplinary assessment.	Request for statutory assessment.
Stage 5: special education forms completed. Record of special education external to ordinary school.	Stage 5: written statement of SEN giving detail of resources provided by LEA.	Written statement of special educational provision.

- ensures access to the full curriculum;
- demonstrates an improvement in self-help personal or social skills;
- demonstrates an improvement in behaviour.

The graduated approach recognizes a range of needs from mild or moderate to severe and complex, and brings increasing levels of expertise if and when necessary. The stages are not meant to be progressive but each assumes a steadily increasing level of professional intervention. Action therefore calls upon increasingly powerful levels of intervention or reduces the intensity of involvement as a child makes progress. The decision regarding initial referral rests largely with the individual early years practitioner and is likely to be partly subjective as the point of referral may vary. The *SEN Toolkit* (DfES 2001c) points out that decisions about which actions are appropriate for which children should be made on an individual basis and should take into account careful assessments of the child, consideration of the child's need for different approaches to learning and the early education setting or school context.

Individual professional judgements are crucial in the entire process and monitoring of individual children's progress is essential. The language of SEN plays an important part in the consequences of assessment and in influencing professional perceptions of, and responses to, children with perceived SEN. Professionals, such as the special educational needs coordinator (SENCO) and the setting manager, are making important judgements and decisions about whether or not children have SEN and how those needs should be met: 'Professionals and their judgements are indispensable to the assessment process for special education, particularly when the assessment leads to statementing' (Galloway *et al.* 1994: 119). Where a child appears not to be making progress either generally or in a specific area of learning, then it may be necessary to present different opportunities or use alternative approaches to learning. Once a decision has been made that ongoing difficulties or failure to make progress amount to a special educational concern, the setting intervenes though *Early Years Action*, or *School Action* in the case of schools. The *Code* makes it clear that specially planned intervention is only necessary if the ongoing difficulties indicate the level of help needed is above that normally available for children in early years settings. In other words, if the early years worker judges the child's expected achievements to be below what could be thought reasonable and some *additional* or *different* action is needed to enable the child to learn more effectively, then Early Years Action is implemented. If, after a period of time, the planned intervention still does not enable the child to make satisfactory progress the SENCO may need to seek advice and support from external support agencies. These could be one or more of the following: GP, health visitor, speech and language therapist, paediatrician, dietician, physiotherapist, educational or clinical psychologist, portage services or local preschool team. The child's provision progresses to forms of intervention involving external specialists which are referred to as *Early Years Action Plus* or *School Action Plus*.

Early Years Action

The primary purpose of Early Years Action appears to be motivated by a desire to help the child progress. This stage is characterized by initial concern, information gathering and if necessary an IEP. The trigger for action is usually concern, supported by evidence, expressed by a practitioner, parent or other professional. The action that follows includes an initial assessment and the collection of information by the SENCO and colleagues. The purpose of gathering information is to reveal the different perceptions of those involved with the child, including the parents, to discover the immediate educational concerns and the wider context of the difficulties. Collecting all known information about the child and seeking new information from the child's parents is an important part of Early Years Action. At first this will be an informal process. Staff and parents should discuss any concerns and observe the child carefully to identify his or her strengths and difficulties, involving the child wherever possible. At the stage of initial concern all the evidence should be considered and a decision made in consultation with the SENCO, staff and parents whether to continue to provide for the child within the normal curriculum framework or to start intervention and place the child on the settings SEN register.

It is very difficult to make judgements about the progress of children in preschool settings and reception classes. As the *Code* (DfES 2001a) acknowledges, this is a period of rapid development and change. Sometimes the transition from home to preschool or nursery to school can be quite daunting. Children may not perform to their full potential for some time. It is important, therefore, to avoid premature judgements and take time to assess children carefully over a period of weeks as they adjust to their new environment. Once a child is settled in to the setting, concern may be triggered if, in spite of appropriate teaching methods, resources and strategies, the child is:

• making little or no progress;
• working at significantly lower levels than other children the same age;
• presenting signs of emotional or behavioural difficulties;

or has:

• sensory or physical difficulties which hinder progress;
• communication or interaction difficulties and needs specific support to access learning.

(DfES 2001a: 4:21)

Through careful observation, assessment and the collecting of relevant information it should be possible to form a profile of a child's levels of performance and identify the areas of development which cause most concern. It is important to build up a picture of the child's strengths and weaknesses without the need to label or categorize the child as 'special'. A child may have one or more areas of difficulty and it is important to decide which is the most likely to hinder progress. Common areas of concern include attention or listening skills (where a child may be observed to be easily distracted, unable to tolerate adult intervention, have difficulty concentrating or completing activities or listening even in a small group) and social skills – for example where a child finds it very difficult to share, take turns or join in group activities. Perhaps interaction with other children or adults is limited and cooperation minimal. In receptive language a child may be seen to have difficulty understanding simple questions, words or instructions. Alternatively, a child may struggle with expressive language and be unable to use words to indicate their needs, become frustrated and need to use gestures to communicate. Some children cause concern as they appear not to be able to engage in simple pretend play or experiment with play materials. They seem unusually disinterested in toys and equipment. Where the problem is related to emotional or behavioural skills the child may be observed to have low self-esteem, or may find it difficult to mange conflict or realize consequences of actions. Sometimes the child displays unpredictable, disruptive and even violent behaviour. He or she may show a negative attitude to learning and to his or her peer group.

Whatever the nature of the concern, once identified the next steps must be planned to meet the needs of the child. Practitioners need to address the most important areas. What is the priority concern? What can the child do now? What does the child need to learn next? The answers will be the target for the child's IEP. As a result, 'special' or extra help may be provided within the 'normal' curriculum framework. This help might incorporate more focused differentiation, individualized programmes and alternative means of accessing the curriculum (e.g. through information and communication technology – ICT – or specific teaching methods). If extra help is to be given then parents should be informed and the problem, the targets and a review date should be recorded:

If it is decided the child is not making adequate progress then staff, SENCO and parents agree the 'action' to be taken and an IEP is devised and provision put in place. When an early years practitioner who works day-to-day with the child, or the SENCO, identifies a child with SEN, they should devise interventions that are *additional to* or *different from* those provided as part of the setting's normal curriculum.

(DfES 2001a: 4:20)

The child's progress should be continually monitored and reviewed at least half termly. At the review the child may continue at this stage with new targets, or may have made enough progress to warrant removal of the special help. If continued concerns are confirmed, the practitioner can then decide to seek advice from external agencies and implement Early Years Action Plus. Here is a step-by-step breakdown of Early Years Action:

- child's learning, behaviour or development gives initial cause for concern;
- staff raise concerns, talk informally to each other and to parents;
- SENCO and staff gather information;
- staff in setting and parents at home observe child;
- note strengths and areas of concern;
- staff, parents and SENCO agree action needed;
- IEP is drawn up to record intervention;
- IEP is implemented for given timescale;
- IEP is reviewed by staff and parents through formal discussion;
- decision is made regarding next steps.

Early Years Action Plus

At this stage, the IEP is still the mechanism for assessment and provision. However, external agencies are consulted to help plan and review the child's progress and devise the targets. The first step is to obtain parental consent to involve outside agencies and this should be put in writing following discussion. Outside specialists visit the setting and observe the child. They offer a range of support and advice – for example, providing more specialist assessments, advice on new or specialist strategies, or suggesting ideas for resources. The SENCO liaises with the specialists, convenes review meetings and invites the child's parents. Again, if by the end of the second review period progress is not satisfactory, a decision may be made as to whether the child should be referred for statutory assessment. There is a continued emphasis on gathering evidence, with assessment becoming a way of 'proving' the child has 'special' needs which demand additional provision.

Developing IEPs

The IEP sets out the nature of the child's difficulty, the special provision, the targets to be achieved within a given time, monitoring arrangements, any help from parents and the review date. It should be used for children at Early Years Action and Early Years Action Plus (or School Action or School Action Plus) and for children with statements of SEN. It identifies and targets areas for action relating to the child's immediate learning needs and any arrangements which may need to be made to help the child make satisfactory progress. It also identifies any human or material resources required. The purpose of the IEP is to reach informed decisions about future learning and teaching. Group education plans (GEPs) may also be formulated – for example, for groups of children whose levels of play or development are noticeably below those of children of similar age.

The IEP can be written by the SENCO, the preschool supervisor or the child's key worker and at Early Years Action Plus this would be in consultation with outside agencies. An IEP should be a straightforward, working document, not simply another piece of bureaucracy. An accessible and understandable IEP serves as a plan and record of what the setting is doing to meet the child's needs. The process of developing IEPs should be manageable and effective. There is no 'correct' or standardized format for an IEP. It may be that a preschool group can adopt the format used in the local area or school. It is important that an IEP is clear and easy to use, easy to read and links with the established plans and routines of the preschool. However, whatever the format, there are certain characteristics which make an IEP effective and which should be included. A good IEP will:

- be brief and action based;
- indicate the child's strengths and current level of achievement;
- identify the nature and extent of the child's learning needs;
- include specific and relevant targets;
- indicate how other adults/parents or carers may be involved;
- note any additional resources or medical needs;
- set dates for review.

A useful starting point is to consider the following four questions:

- Assessment: what can Jane do now?
- Targets set: what do we want Jane to achieve next?
- Strategy: how shall we help her do this?
- Review: what has Jane achieved?

Targets should be few in number, expressed positively and not set a child up for failure. It is important to focus on short-term goals and specific objectives rather than general aims. As the sample IEPs show (see Tables 3.2 to 3.5), the targets should be specific as to exactly what it is hoped the child will achieve in a given period of time. If the general aim is, say, to 'improve social skills', then the target could be written as 'play cooperatively with one other child in the role-play area for ten minutes twice a week'. Similarly, rather than write 'improve behaviour', the target could be 'sit for ten minutes without disrupting story time, keeping hands and feet to himself'. The SMART target is a commonly used and successful approach:

- **S**pecific – agreed with parents, all staff and where appropriate the child.
- **M**easurable – clear expected outcomes.
- **A**chievable – given the level of support available.
- **R**ecorded – on the IEP.
- **T**ime defined – record the date by which you expect the child to achieve the target.

The IEP provides a focus for those involved to work together towards a common goal for the child. The involvement of all staff in devising and implementing IEPs could encourage early years professionals to reflect on their own practice, encourage differentiation and self-reflection and promote the use of a wider range of teaching techniques with all children. If a child is at Early Years Action Plus, the IEP should also include details of which outside agencies are involved and their role in helping the child achieve the target. Of course, it is essential to involve parents and record the ways in which they may help the child at home. The IEP targets and strategies must be inclusive and enable children to access the curriculum rather than be separated from it.

The IEP must have a clear timescale and refer to the action to be taken at the review stage. The review focuses on the outcome of the action taken and should consider the progress made towards the targets. It should take into account the parents' and child's viewpoints and establish any further action to be taken in meeting the child's individual needs. At an Early Years Action review those involved will need to decide whether the child is making significantly good progress, in which case special intervention would be withdrawn, although informal monitoring would continue. If the child is making good progress he or she could remain at Early Years Action with revised or new targets. If the targets have not been achieved those involved need to consider why this may be so. Were the targets too difficult and should they be broken down

Table 3.2 An IEP for Early Years Action

Name:	Simon Smith	IEP No.:	1
M/F:	M	Stage:	Early Years Action
DOB:	1/4/2000	Started:	4/10/03
Placement:	Happydays Nursery	Review date:	November 04

Goals:
To reduce inappropriate behaviours
To develop social skills

What: target(s)	How: strategies/activities/resources	Who/where/when
1 To understand the rule of 'no hitting'	Use of a visual reminder, at beginning of session as reminder and when hitting during session	All nursery staff in all activities. Visual symbol to reinforce. Use STOP signal. Remove from activity if continues to hit out
2 To respond to the instruction STOP	Use of a visual signal	Adults to use when inappropriate behaviour occurs. Avoid lengthy explanations. Remove from activity/time out, if behaviour reoccurs
3 To be able to share toys with an adult and one or two other children	Adult modelling appropriate language, my turn, your turn, wait. Practise sharing, asking for a turn and taking turns. Comment on good sharing etc.	Children can also use All adults during free play activities
4 To ask for a turn/toy appropriately	Asking appropriately (e.g. train please). Activities could include: construction, taking turns to build a tower, sharing trains by taking turns to run a train around a track. Use STOP when fighting occurs in free play	In small group activity twice a week for 15–20 minutes

into smaller steps? Was the strategy appropriate for the child's needs? Was the timing of the additional input suitable? Was the support frequent enough to provide for practise of the task? Alternatively, if after two review periods the special help has not resulted in satisfactory progress and the child is still significantly behind other children, the setting needs to seek external advice and Early Year Action Plus implemented.

Table 3.3 An IEP for Early Years Action Plus

Name:	Thomas Tucker	Start date: April 2003		Stage:	Early Years Action Plus
Areas of concern:	Behaviour			Year group:	Nursery
Class teacher:	Mary Hubbard			Review date:	Spring 2004
Support by:	Katie Fisher			Support began:	January 2003

Targets to be achieved	Achievement criteria	Possible resources/ techniques	Possible class strategies	Ideas for support/assistant	Outcome
1 To be able to negotiate his own needs with another child in a free play situation	Observed by staff involved on three occasions	Role play. Free play situations	Adults to model negotiation skills. Support Thomas to negotiate verbally. Praise appropriate social skills	Talk through situations as they arise with Thomas. Help him to apply situations	Achieved 7/7/03
2 To listen quietly when others are speaking and wait for his turn to speak	Observed to listen without interruption for two minutes on three separate occasions	Object to pass around as a signal for permission to speak	Circle time activities. Class discussions	Talk about the importance of listening to others. Praise/ reward achievement	Working towards 7/7/03
3 To speak at an appropriate volume/ pitch during group sessions each date	Thomas is heard to speak at an appropriate volume/pitch in group situations each day	Tape recorder. Role-play. Music sessions singing/playing instruments loudly and quietly. Read stories using different volumes	Encourage Thomas to speak at the appropriate volume/pitch. Play noisy/quiet games. Read stories using different volumes	Play games involving different volumes. Tape record own voices	Working towards 7/7/03
4 Withdraw funded helper involvement to encourage Thomas' independence	Thomas to maintain appropriate social skills and ability to stay on task independently		Helper to monitor – intervene if needed		

Parent/carers need to: Encourage Thomas to negotiate his needs with appropriate verbal responses. Encourage Thomas to wait for others to finish speaking before he begins. Model appropriate volume when talking to Thomas. Praise appropriate use of volume

Child needs to: Try to apply negotiation skills. Wait for his turn to speak. Listen to other people. Use voice appropriately

Table 3.4 An IEP for a child with learning difficulties

Name:	Peter Piper	IEP No.:	2
M/F:	M	Stage:	Early Years Action Plus
DOB:	22/10/99	Started:	7/12/02
Placement:	Happydays Nursery	Review Date:	January 04

Goals:

To encourage Peter to make (and sequence) independent choices of activities

To enable Peter to understand routines

To encourage Peter to sit, listen and join in appropriately during short group activities (e.g. for stories and 'sharing' times with his peer)

What: target(s), including success criteria	How: strategies/ activities/resources	Who/where/when	Progress
1 To choose three play activities at the start of each session – the first, next and last. (*Success criteria: Peter can do this at least twice per week*)	Using a selection of picture cue cards which Peter chooses from – then displaying his three choices on a board/wall so that they can be clearly referred to	Upon arrival at the start of each session – helped by an adult assistant	
2 To choose a quiet activity out of a pre-prepared activity box. (*Success criteria: playing independently and then returning to group for five minutes – sitting quietly*)	At the start of any 'key worker' time, which involves sitting down and listening for over 20 minutes, Peter is encouraged to choose a quiet game (Peter is brought to rejoin the group for the last five minutes). A designated box ('Peter's box') is prepared for Peter (this could also be done at home) filled with jigsaws (e.g. transport jigsaws), favourite books etc. for his use at these times	Box is placed in a known area to Peter, away from the group activity, so that it is not a distraction. Any adult can direct Peter to this box at these 'key worker' times. He must then be encouraged to sit quietly upon returning to the group	
3 To sit still on the carpet and listen with two other children – in a listening game (e.g. sound lotto). (*Success criteria: five minutes*)	Using picture cue cards for good sitting, listening, looking and being quiet. Using a carpet square/cushion/ shape to establish 'personal space'. Using a timer (e.g. an egg timer/ cooker timer)	Listening games with two other children and adult (twice a week, maximum of ten minutes) OR at home with mum/dad	

Table 3.5 A IEP for a child with emotional difficulties

Name:	Lucy Lockett	IEP No.:	1
M/F:	F	Stage:	Early Years Action Plus
DOB:	15/5/00	Started:	Dec 02
Placement:	Happydays Nursery	Review Date:	April 03

Goals:

Accessing the curriculum:	Lucy to engage in a range of adult-directed activities.
Personal and social education:	Turn-taking skills. Lucy to participate in a small group activity (one adult, three children) responding appropriately.
Gross motor skills:	Lucy to use a variety of outdoor apparatus.

What: target(s)	**How:** strategies/activities/resources	**Who/where/when**
To focus on adult-directed play activity for five minutes (adult choosing)	Adult to ask/tell Lucy to join the activity and to model play and language. Gradually fade the support so Lucy is left to finish/continue the activity independently (e.g. 'I just want you to carry on with this while I just …')	All staff. Targeted activity. Change activity frequently
Lucy to take part in turn-taking activities with an adult and another child	Starting with one adult and one child, use high interest activity (e.g. bubbles, brick tower building). Move on to other activities. Lucy to demonstrate an understanding of the social rules by participating appropriately, waiting for her turn	One adult and one child. Five-minute sessions to be practised daily
To negotiate the steps without the aid of an adult hand To pedal a bike	The wooden steps outside. Encourage Lucy to go onto the first step on her own and then hold her hand for the others. When she is on the last step, encourage her to make the last step herself. Increase the number of steps up first before working on the steps on the way down.	Staff outside to practise the activity twice daily Another bike has been found that Lucy can feel more confident with Sources: Early Years Centre Toy Library

Request for statutory assessment and written statement

If the help given by the early education setting under Early Years Action Plus is still not sufficient to enable the child to make progress, the staff in the setting need to consider whether to make a request for statutory multidisciplinary assessment. Parents, schools and early education settings in receipt of government funding to provide early education currently have the right to request an assessment for 4- and 5-year-olds but after September 2004 this should be extended to cover 3-year-olds. This is where consultation with parents and external agencies is crucial. The information on the child's learning difficulty and the evidence of the special educational provision made at Early Years Action and Early Years Action Plus will form the basis of the LEA's consideration of whether a statutory assessment is necessary. During this stage, findings from individual professionals are considered by the LEA in order to write a 'statement' which will allocate extra resources to the individual child. There is a significant shift as the LEA becomes the decision maker, responsible at administrative level for providing the resources to meet the child's needs. Only where the conclusion is that the child's needs are so complex as to be long-term or the specialist early intervention cannot be provided within the setting's normal resources is the LEA likely to conclude that an assessment is necessary.

The final stage of the graduated model of assessment incorporates a written statement of the child's SEN made by the LEA. The procedures for children over 2 but under compulsory school age are the same as for children of school age. The main grounds for the decision to write a statement are that the special educational provision cannot reasonably be provided within the normal resources of a mainstream setting school in the area. Again, the point at which this decision is made can vary from area to area and indeed case to case. The outcome at this point could include additional human or material resources in the mainstream school or placement in a special school or unit. Staff in early years settings should refer to the criteria for statutory assessment of children under compulsory school age and over 2 in the *Code of Practice* (DfES 2001a) for further guidance.

Children under 2 are normally referred to the LEA by the health service and are likely to have a health problem that has caused concern from an early age. The LEA may make an assessment of the child's SEN with parental consent and *must* make such an assessment if the parent requests it. Statements will be rare for children under 2 and the assessment need not follow the statutory procedures applicable to children over 2. First, individual programmes of support such as a peripatetic service for children with hearing or visual impairment will be considered. Centre-based provision may also be offered if available. For children under 3 with complex needs, special educational provision might also include full- or part-time attendance at a nursery or preschool group, or a home-based learning programme involving visiting teachers and parents in teaching the child. If a child under 5 has received considerable support without a statement it is important for those working with the child to request statutory assessment if his or her needs are such that support will be needed on starting school. However, making decisions about the transition from the preschool setting to full-time school can prove problematic and are dependent on the perceptions of the professionals involved.

Professional perceptions

The relationship between the procedures, their purposes and the consequences for pupils perceived as having SEN is not straightforward. The *Code* (DfES 2001a) provides a framework for professionals to feel that they are acting in the best interests of the child, particularly if there is an expected resource outcome. Assessment in the *Code of Practice* is seen to be motivated by concern to help the individual child progress but at the same time this assessment is used to identify approximately more than a fifth of the school population as 'special'. Some commentators argue that the concept of 'need', and many of the decisions associated with that concept, may be based on individual, often subjective judgements of professionals, which are then presented as objective, based on the beliefs, interests and needs of those who have the power to make decisions (Vincent *et al.* 1996). The two cases below demonstrate the tentative nature of decision making and demonstrate that sometimes whether a child ends up in special or mainstream education can simply be the result of luck rather than judgement.

Tom: in nursery year

Tom was diagnosed by a doctor as 'autistic' with associated speech and language difficulties. He attended a mainstream nursery without support. As he approached 4 years questions arose as to whether he should attend a mainstream primary school or segregated special provision. Professionals unanimously agreed that he needed segregated special provision. The assumption was that full-time attendance in a special language unit, several miles away from his home village, would be in Tom's best interests because it offered favourable adult to child ratios and specialist speech and language support. The speech therapist reported that 'Tom would benefit from being in a small-class teaching situation with teachers who specialize in the education of children with communication disorders, and where there is the availability of individual/small-group teaching plus speech and language therapy'. A further report from the head of the speech and language team also supported the view that Tom needed special rather than mainstream provision: 'a class where the teachers have specialized knowledge and expertise in working with children who present with autistic spectrum difficulties, plus an environment where there is availability of speech and language therapy'. However, the language unit was full, so Tom joined the reception class at his local village school where he thrived with 15 hours of support a week.

David: towards end of nursery year

David's mother thought he needed to attend a special school: 'I feel that David requires one to one care, a school that can give this. Three Castles Special School would seem the only suitable course of action for him'. The senior clinical medical officer supported this view wholeheartedly: 'David needs to attend a special school where he would get attention on a one-to-one basis'. The medical officer implied that one-to-one support would not be made available in a mainstream school. Similarly, David's preschool teacher inferred that it would be in his best interest to be among the best in a special school rather than bottom in a mainstream reception class. As with Tom, the suggestion was that mainstream schooling would not cater for David's needs: 'I would have great concerns about David adjusting to a large group. I feel that a school that can skilfully work with children with such needs, where David would be among the best, would be appropriate'. This suggests that David may have coped in mainstream but would find it difficult to adjust to a large group. But not everyone agreed. By contrast, the educational psychologist's report recommended 'access to the full mainstream curriculum appropriate to David's age'. Shortly after his statement was written, a couple who lived only a few houses away from a village school adopted David. This involved a move across the LEA boundary. After consulting the educational psychologist, his adoptive parents enrolled him at the local school. A few months later, he was allocated an LSA for ten hours a week and started full-time in the same reception class, sharing the same assistant as Tom.

Conclusion

It is clear by looking at the graduated procedure that children very quickly become categories, identified as somehow different from the norm. First, a child is in one of two broad groups: those with and those without statements. Second, within these groups children on the 'special needs register' are moved in and out of Early Years Action and Early Years Action Plus. Third, within each stage children are classified into more subsets of group or individual 'difficulties', sometimes referred to under a column 'reason for referral' on the SEN register. The graduated model of assessment may yet serve to accentuate differences and reinforce often negative group identities. This reinforces the idea that SEN are an *individual* deficit. Children are subjected to continuous monitoring and their feelings about their own self-worth, identities and experiences may be shaped by the formal assessment procedures and by informal daily interactions within the educational setting. As a result of being processed through Early Years Action and Early Years Action Plus children may be moved progressively further away from 'normal' into 'special' educational provision. This 'spiral of separation' gives a whole section of the population what Fulcher calls an 'identity of difference' which 'contains or institutes a political logic of exclusion' (1990: 351). Ostensibly, the situation appears to be straightforward: 'If they're struggling within that peer group why not give them the help? I don't think they know they're labelled. You don't tell them they're special needs do you? You just work on them.' This assistant had already given a separate identity to the group of 4-year-olds which she had been allocated to support. Although not explicitly told that 'they' were 'special needs' the implication is that these children hadn't enough sense to realize that they were 'different' and as long as they were not actually informed of this fact the end justified the means. Unless we examine our professional perceptions, whole groups of children can be lumped together and assigned a 'special needs' label.

There are key conceptual and practical issues concerning questions of categorization and segregation in the early years which still need to be addressed. Assessment is not merely confined to issues of provision, as the broader social consequences of being identified as 'special' could be lifelong. Categories and labels tend to have an effect independent of that for which they are intended. It is important for those working in early years settings to evaluate the potential impact of the stages in the *Code of Practice* and the effect that assessment procedures may have on the way children are perceived by others and perceive themselves. The curious paradox is that for some children, becoming boxed into labelled compartments is seen as a positive step. In a climate of competition for resources, parental pressure groups tend to represent particular categories – for example, autism, Asperger's syndrome and dyslexia. Success is marked by an acceptance that the child is distinguished from other children, in that he or she fits into one or even more than one particular category. The label is seen as an acceptable explanation for a child's difficulties, a means of gaining recognition and extra help.

The early identification and assessment procedures in the *Code of Practice* still focus on how a child's needs can be met within the context of his or her group education and care, rather than on how those needs are created or exacerbated by interactions or circumstances that take place within the school itself. As Galloway *et al.* contend, 'assessment all too easily becomes divorced from wider considerations of the school' and concentrates on 'what is wrong with the child and the family rather than on ways in which children can be taught effectively within the ordinary classroom' (1994: 155).

Assessment is a process often dominated by bureaucracy and procedural concerns. The focus is on administration and allocation of resources, with little attention to structural responses. The emphasis is on the individual child's 'private' problems rather than any consideration of the 'public' political, social or educational context (Tomlinson 1982; Fulcher 1990; Barton and Oliver 1992). The introduction of IEPs into early education settings provides official sanction for certain children to be treated differently. Unless early years practitioners are made aware of these issues, intentionally or otherwise, the graduated model of assessment may create a system whereby children are being labelled and perceived as somehow 'different' from the majority of their peer group at progressively earlier ages. We need to take care that the principles of early years education are not undermined by an unwieldy and fragmented system of assessment and provision. Ultimately, an inclusive model of assessment is needed which is appropriate for all children and not restricted to pupils thought to have SEN.

4

Developing inclusive policy and practice

Inclusive education is a consequence of policies based on equal opportunities – that is, no discrimination on the grounds of race, gender, class, disability or learning difficulty.

(CSIE 1999: 10)

This chapter focuses on the development of inclusion policies in early education settings. The writing of policies is becoming a familiar task in early education settings these days, and schools and early years settings in receipt of government funding for nursery education are required by law to devise and implement a policy for meeting SEN, that is, a policy on their provision for children with disabilities or learning difficulties. The *Code of Practice* (DfES 2001a: 4.3) confirms this, stating that, 'All early education providers delivering government funded nursery education are expected to have a written SEN policy'. It goes on to list the settings that '*must* have a written SEN policy' (1:23, original emphasis) as settings in receipt of government funding for early education, including approved childminder networks, maintained nursery schools, community, foundation and voluntary schools, community and foundation special schools, city academies, city technology colleges and city colleges for the technology of the arts. The *Code of Practice* (DfES 2001a: 1.24, original emphasis) adds that 'The policy *must* contain the information as set out in the Education (Special Educational Needs) (Information) (England) Regulations 1999 at annex A, or in the case of early education settings ... as set out in the conditions of grant'. All registered providers must have a written SEN policy, details must be published to parents and made available to the Office for Standards in Education (Ofsted) inspector. Unregistered preschool providers must also satisfy their LEA that these measures are in place before they can be registered (DfES 2002).

The chapter begins by exploring the importance of policy development and the rationale behind writing an inclusive SEN policy. The rest of the chapter provides detailed guidance on reviewing your current SEN policy and developing an inclusive policy. The chapter promotes the whole-school or whole-setting approach to policy development, in order to make inclusion a high profile issue for all early years workers. A sample policy and extracts from various policies are provided to illustrate the type of information that should be included. It is important to remember that early education settings vary according to size, resources and organization. Your policy not only needs to meet the legal requirements but also to reflect your setting's unique circumstances, interests, specialisms, principles and working practices.

Rationale for devising an inclusion policy

A policy is a statement of philosophy, intent, strategy and current practice. It should actually make a difference to the quality of teaching and learning, reflecting the aspirations and practices of the whole setting. It is a matter of principle and not just a technical exercise. Clark *et al.* (1990) describe practice as the 'active reinterpretation' of policy within individual contexts. They suggest that through the interaction between policy and practice a process of learning and growth may take place. Hence the *Code*'s requirement for a SEN policy should be seen as giving rise to an opportunity for early years workers to review current practice and move towards developing more inclusive cultures and philosophies. However, the official guidance on what a SEN policy should cover does not necessarily guarantee an 'inclusive' approach – in other words, one which will include all children whatever their needs. It is no easy task to change attitudes and working practices. As 'the SEN policy should be seen in the context of equal opportunities and should be designed to promote inclusion' (DfES 2002: 50) it is paramount that all staff should be involved in policy development as you cannot assume that there will be a consensus among all early years practitioners on values or ethos, or indeed on inclusion.

Policy development is commonly associated with accountability. Certainly, Ofsted inspectors will want to comment on the effectiveness or otherwise of your SEN policy and practice. The inspector is required to assess how well the setting meets the needs of children with SEN and has regard to the *Code of Practice*. Being able to provide a clear and current written policy which is implemented in practice by all staff is obviously a good starting point. Parents are also entitled to information on their role in the assessment and decision-making process and it is important to write the policy in a user-friendly way that can be understood by parents and outside agencies as well as staff in the setting. The supporting criteria for the inspection of full daycare and childminding for children under 8 also insist that a registered person provides a written statement about special needs which is consistent with current legislation and guidance on SEN and disabilities, and is made available to parents.

However, writing a policy is not only concerned with external demands, it is about internal processes and procedures. Importantly, discussion of a policy and consultation should be a catalyst for improving teaching and learning for all children including those with SEN. A policy should form a flexible and useful framework for developing and implementing inclusive practices within your setting. It could be argued that in a truly inclusive environment a separate SEN policy may not be necessary at all and the policy, practice and philosophy of inclusion should permeate all policies and all aspects of the life of the setting. A policy on play, for example, might include some reference to accessibility for children with SEN or disabilities. The policy on assessment should incorporate all children, not only those with SEN. The policy on working with parents should incorporate reference to parents of children with SEN. However, for the purposes of clarity, initially at least, the inclusion or SEN policy is expected to be a separate and public document.

The skill in writing policies is to get the main points across to the reader briefly. Think carefully about the language you use. Policies which are kept short and to the point are likely to be more effective than those which are dense, lengthy, difficult to read and to use. However, the SEN or inclusion policy does require a certain amount of information and a lengthier document may be necessary. Clarity and readability for the intended audience are important and more detailed guidance on aspects of day-to-day practice for those directly working with the children could be included as separate appendices. Appendices might include contact details for external support agencies, pro formas for correspondence and record keeping, assessment materials or a list of resources. It is important to avoid (or explain) terms or jargon such as 'differentiation' or 'external agencies' as well as acronyms such as LEA. Alternatively, a shorter version or summary could be written for parents with the full policy made available on request. Although not legally entitled to have a role in devising the policy it may be helpful to invite parents to comment. Overall, the policy needs to be long enough to ensure shared understandings and expectations within and beyond those working with the children.

The policy should establish the ethos of the setting, articulate its commitment to inclusion and celebrate its achievements in meeting the needs of children with individual requirements. Following the original *Code* (DfE 1994) a report from Ofsted (1996) found that not all schools included in their brochure a reference to SEN policy, or in some cases it was very brief. In other cases, schools were reluctant to advertise the fact that they had a significant number of SEN pupils or extensive provision for those pupils. The report also found it was unusual for parents' views to be canvassed in the formulation of the policy. Policies rarely included details of staff expertise. Instead they tended to emphasize the administrative procedures and practices but not how these would improve educational provision in the broader sense of offering a more inclusive curriculum.

It is important for parents to understand from the outset the setting's attitude towards children with SEN. Reference to the setting's ethos in the parents' initial information booklet can be short but explicitly establish your philosophy on inclusion. The example below clearly indicates to parents the importance the setting attaches to meeting the needs of all its children:

> We believe that Busy Bees exists to provide life's main opportunities for our children. These opportunities come from an ethos and curriculum that provide maximum learning opportunities for each individual child, no matter what their particular needs may be ... Our vision is to create a caring, secure and stimulating environment in which each child is recognized as an individual and where self-esteem and self-discipline are positively developed and achievement is celebrated.

As described in Chapter 5, the SENCO is responsible for the day-to-day operation of the SEN policy and research into the original *Code* found SENCOs were shouldering much of the responsibility alone (Ofsted 1996; Crowther *et al.* 1997). Nevertheless, as the table of roles and responsibilities (Table 4.1) shows, all early years workers are responsible for the policy's implementation in terms of developing an inclusive environment and enabling children access the curriculum to achieve their potential. Therefore, the policy needs to be written to reflect this collective responsibility, incorporating the views of all staff rather than just the

SENCO or the setting manager. Involving all staff in discussions about the inclusion of children with SEN will give them a sense of shared ownership, avoiding potential misunderstandings and allaying any fears, apprehensions and anxieties. Staff also need to feel the policy will help them in their role and that they will be supported in implementing it.

Reviewing current practice

A useful starting point is to review your current policy and practice. It is not automatic that a completely new policy needs to be developed. For some settings it may be a matter of evaluating the current policy and making amendments where necessary. In some cases, however, SEN policies, if they exist at all, were written some time ago, while other settings have adopted a 'wholesale' policy produced *en masse* for preschool groups and yet others are simply not implementing their policy in practice. For the majority, developing policy is an opportunity to reappraise and make a fresh start. Given the changing nature of the whole area, starting with a clean sheet could prove to be a useful exercise. Two complementary processes will occur. First, you will need to identify your current position – in other words, where you are now. Second, you will need to consider where you want to be at a specified point in the future. You can then decide on the action to be taken and produce an action plan similar to the one shown in Table 4.2. The starting point will be reviewing and discussing the existing policy and amending or revising it to fulfil the requirements of the *Code* (DfES 2001a) and the conditions of grant which state that for early years settings the policy must incorporate:

- a clear statement as to what the policy is seeking to achieve and how it relates to the *Code of Practice* and its associated guidance on the identification and assessment of SEN;
- the name of the person responsible in the setting for cocoordinating day-to-day provision of education for pupils with SEN, whether or not that person carries the formal title of SENCO;
- support available within the setting for children with SEN, including facilities for increasing access for children who are disabled;
- arrangements for reviewing, monitoring and evaluating the effectiveness of the setting's SEN provision;
- arrangements for working in partnership with parents, taking into account the wishes of the child;

Table 4.1 Roles and responsibilities in mainstream schools and early education settings

In maintained mainstream schools	In early education settings
The governing body should, in cooperation with the headteacher, determine the school's general policy and approach to provision for children with SEN, establish the appropriate staffing and funding arrangements and maintain a general oversight of the school's work	**The setting's management group** should work with practitioners to determine the setting's general policy and approach to provision for children with SEN
The governing body may appoint a committee to take a particular interest in and closely monitor the school's work on behalf of children with SEN **The governing body** must report to parents annually on the school's policy on SEN	
The headteacher has responsibility for the day-to-day management of all aspects of the school's work, including provision for children with SEN. The headteacher should keep the governing body fully informed and also work closely with the school's SENCO or team	**The head of the setting** has responsibility for the day-to-day management of all aspects of the setting's work, including provision for children with SEN. The head of the setting should keep the management group fully informed and also work closely with the SENCO
All teaching and non-teaching staff should be involved in the development of the school's SEN policy and be fully aware of the school's procedures for identifying, assessing and making provision for pupils with SEN	**All practitioners** should be involved in the development of the SEN policy and be fully aware of the procedures for identifying, assessing and making provision for children with SEN
The SENCO (or team), working closely with the headteacher, senior management and fellow teachers, should be closely involved in the strategic development of the SEN policy and provision. The SENCO has responsibility for day-to-day operation of the school's SEN policy and for coordinating provision for pupils with SEN, particularly through *School Action* and *School Action Plus.*	**The SENCO**, working closely with the head of the setting and colleagues, has responsibility for the day to day operation of the setting's SEN policy and for coordinating provision for children with SEN, particularly through *Early Years Action* and *Early Years Action Plus.*

Source: adapted from DfES (2001a: 1.39)

Table 4.2 Action Plan for inclusion policy development

Goals:
1 To produce an updated special needs policy which contains all the information requirements of the *Code of Practice*
2 To involve all staff in the development of policy

Action to be taken	*By whom?*	*By when?*
Time in staff meeting to brainstorm special needs policy objectives	All nursery staff	Next staff meeting
Job description of SENCO to be developed	Jane (nursery manager) and Jo (SENCO)	By 31 May
Draft register established	Jo working with all staff on an audit of special needs	By July
All features which enable access for the disabled to be listed	Jo with some advice from Pete (teacher at local special school)	By July
Staff to receive in-house training about their duties and responsibilities	Jo supported by Jane	Next full meeting of governing body
Screening and assessment materials to be reviewed. Feedback to staff about procedures to adopt	Jane supported by Jo	By July
LEA documentation for the staged approach to be adopted	All staff. Implementation of IEPs to be monitored by Jo	Start of autumn term having trialled some in summer term
Parents to be informed about their rights and responsibilities	Jane	Start of autumn term
All external support services to be listed. Reference directory in staff room	Jane	Start of autumn term
Policy adopted by staff and management committee	Jo and Jane in discussion with staff and management committee	By July

Source: adapted from Luton (1995)

- procedures for resolving complaints about SEN provision;
- a description of links with local support services, agencies and educational settings in the area.

(DfES 2002: Annex 4)

Suggestions are made later in this chapter as to what could be included under each of these sections. Small working parties could be established as part of the review process and may include parents. They could consider questions such as – Does your policy 'have regard' to the *Code of Practice*? Does your practice reflect the policy? Is the policy and practice effective in meeting the needs of all children?

In your discussions you would need to explore the extent to which all early years workers in your setting have a shared philosophy. You should consider any aspects of practice that are not clear in the existing policy and comment on the effectiveness of the current provision for assessing, observing and recording children's needs. Policy review and development is a continuous process. The questions below (adapted from Luton 1995) provide a useful starting point for your review. You could then draw up a list of changes which need to be made.

Ask yourself the following key questions:

- Does your setting have a clear set of objectives for meeting the needs of children with SEN?
- Have the objectives been reviewed and are they consistent with the *Code of Practice*?
- Have the objectives been shared with all staff?
- Have you an identified SEN co-coordinator?
- Is the SENCO job description in line with the *Code of Practice*?
- Are staff responsibilities at each stage of assessment clear?
- Are there admission arrangements for children with SEN with and without statements in the SEN policy?
- Do you have an agreed system of record keeping and documentation?
- Do you have a system for involving parents, children and external agencies in the planning and review process?
- Do you have a programme for staff development in line with the *Code of Practice*?
- What have you done to reduce barriers to exclusion?

Apart from the mechanics of policy development, the Centre for Studies on Inclusive Education (CSIE) (1999) suggest you consider key questions relating to attitudes: Do you value all children equally? Are the educational aims for all children the same? How do you enable all children to experience success? Do you see parents as crucial to a child's education? The CSIE (1999: 12) suggest that you could set targets for developing inclusion in six key areas:

● changing attitudes inside and beyond the setting;
● designing and publishing a new policy for inclusion;
● acquiring resources to ensure policy is implemented;
● making the environment accessible;
● developing staff expertise;
● developing inclusive activities.

The next section provides a detailed framework for planning and organizing your policy development. It incorporates the legal require-ments and the order is largely based on headings in the guidance for early education and childcare settings in Warwickshire (WCC 2001) with suggestions as to the type of information to be included in each section. Of course, additional inclusions, (e.g. provision for the more able not officially categorized under the SEN umbrella) can be chosen to be incorporated into your policy. The important thing is that the practices within the written policy need to be manageable in a day-to-day situa-tion.

Inclusion policy framework

Section 1: basic information about the setting's special educational provision

This section should include a brief statement about the aims, principles and objectives of the policy and will set the tone for the rest of the policy. It should set out the setting's philosophy and the basic beliefs shared by the staff in relation to the inclusion of children with SEN and/or dis-abilities. The examples shown illustrate how this section can promote an inclusive approach by placing learning support within the context of provision for all children in the setting and fixing responsibility from the outset as an integral rather than separate part of all teaching and learning.

Extract 1: Triangle Nursery Policy

Aims and objectives
Our nursery aims to be an inclusive nursery. This means that equality of opportunity must be a reality for our children. We make

this a reality through the attention we pay to the different groups of children within our setting:

- girls and boys;
- children who need support to learn English as an additional language;
- children with SEN;
- more able children;
- any children who are at risk of exclusion;
- minority ethnic and faith groups.

We achieve educational inclusion by continually reviewing what we do, by asking ourselves these key questions:

- Do all our children achieve as much as they can?
- Are there differences in the achievement of different groups of children?
- What are we doing for those children who we know are not achieving their best?
- Are our actions effective?

Extract 2: Newlands Infant School

We seek to be an inclusive school by:

- using the SEN review procedures to identify any barriers in the way of pupil progress and planning appropriate and reasonable action;
- ensuring that all pupils have appropriate learning targets which are challenging;
- valuing the diversity of all our pupils, of which SEN pupils are a natural part;
- looking for opportunities within the curriculum to raise SEN issues;
- seeking to make provision for SEN within routine class arrangements wherever possible;
- seeking opportunities for pupils with SEN to work with other pupils;
- encouraging pupils with SEN to play/socialize with other pupils;
- developing links with special schools to extend all pupils' experience of diversity.

Edgington (1998) suggests that you should begin by considering the rationale for the policy. This process addresses what the 'why' questions. For an inclusion policy these might include questions such as: Why do we need an inclusion policy? Why do we need to work with parents? Why do we need to consider admissions? The policy could perhaps include a well-chosen quote – for example, from the *Code*. It should provide the name of the SENCO who must be committed to inclusion and give an outline of the SENCO's responsibilities.

Extract 3: Oakfield Primary School

The SENCO (Tina French) works with the senior management team of the school to:

- identify the pattern of needs across the school;
- establish the most cost effective means of meeting these needs;
- allocate support to groups of pupils and individual pupils, including those with statements of SEN;
- ensure that support is allocated to pupils on a fair and equitable basis;
- monitor the progress made by pupils with SEN;
- evaluate the effectiveness of provision for SEN;
- ensure that support staff, including teaching assistants, work within the framework of school policy and practice.

The SENCO's responsibilities could be taken straight from the *Code of Practice*. If the role is shared it is important to make lines of responsibility clear and make other staff aware of their collective responsibilities. The policy should contain information on admission arrangements for all children with and without statements.

The policy should also outline if the setting has any specialist resources or staff expertise – for example, someone on the staff may be able to use sign language. Mention any specialist facilities such as ramps or soft play equipment, ensuring partial accessibility is phrased positively rather than as a barrier to inclusion. Specialist facilities should be regarded as an asset for all children, not just certain sections of the setting.

Extract 4: The Vale Playgroup

Some children in our playgroup may have disabilities and consequently need additional resources. The management is committed to providing an environment that allows all children full access to all areas of learning. All our internal entrances are wide enough for wheelchair access and the designated points of entry for our playgroup also allow wheelchair access.

You need to identify arrangements for considering complaints about SEN provision. The policy should state the procedures for recording and acting upon parental concerns and for involving parents when a concern is first expressed. You may not only receive complaints from the parents of the child with SEN but also from other parents – for example, about a child's presence in the setting. Often, complaints may not be an accusation of poor practice but an expression of concern. However, a clear procedure for all staff to follow is essential in the unlikely event of any serious concern.

Section 2: arrangements for identification, assessment and provision for children with SEN

This section should provide an overview of what actually happens in practice through the graduated assessment model – in other words, arrangements and resources for children with difficulties whether they be temporary setbacks, long-term impairments or illness, or if the children are at Early Years Action or Early Years Action Plus. This section of the policy is concerned with providing guidelines for practices and procedures and addresses the 'how' questions (Edgington 1998): for example, how you will ensure the purposes of the policy are achieved. Here you could outline the actual procedures the setting will follow in order to achieve the outcomes. Section 2 should inform the reader about how a child will be identified, assessed and provided for on a day-to-day basis within the setting. This section would also include reference to the record keeping for children on the SEN register, how IEPs are planned and reviewed and how children and parents are involved in reviews. It would take account of arrangements for providing access to the foundation stage curriculum – for example, you could explain the differentiated levels of support available within your setting. Overall, this section should embrace the commitment and will of the setting to enable children with SEN to participate fully in the work, play and social experiences available to all children within the setting. The extract from Dalemeadow Nursery highlights this point.

Extract 5: Dalemeadow Nursery

Staff ensure that children:

- feel secure and know that their contributions are valued;
- appreciate and value the differences they see in others;
- take responsibility for their own actions;
- participate safely in clothing that is appropriate to their religious beliefs;
- are taught in groupings that allow them all to experience success;
- use materials that reflect a range of social and cultural backgrounds, without stereotyping;
- have common curriculum experiences that allow for a range of different learning styles;
- have challenging targets that enable them to succeed;
- are encouraged to participate fully, regardless of disabilities or medical needs.

Section 3: information about staffing policies and partnerships with parents and external agencies

This section should promote a commitment to improving the knowledge and skills of staff. It could outline opportunities for professional development such as where to access information relating to local training events, courses or conferences. It should highlight the ways in which the setting liaises with external agencies – for example, from education, health or social services, and how these services support the inclusion process. An appendix could contain contact details and explain the roles of local support services.

The process of working in partnership with parents could also be in this section. It might comprise of three aspects: information, access and involvement. This might consist of providing information about the support available in the setting and in the locality, with useful addresses of local and national voluntary organizations which might provide information or advice. It could describe how parents' views are incorporated into their child's assessment and provision. You could provide access to information in community languages or on tape. This section should also indicate your setting's links with any preschool networks such as the Preschool Learning Alliance or National Private Day Nurseries Association, and any liaison with other educational settings, including other preschools or primary schools.

Section 4: criteria for evaluating success of the policy

In this section you will need to identify who will monitor and review the policy and in what timescale. How will an eye be kept on its implementation and whose responsibility will it be to see if it is being implemented in practice and observe the impact? There should be a planned programme to review the policy in the light of any changes in legislation, inspection demands, staffing or accommodation. The purpose of the evaluation will be to consider how far the policy has been effective in meeting its aims and objectives in practice and to provide feedback to those involved. Are staff and parents well informed, involved and clear about their roles and responsibilities? Does the IEP planning and review process work smoothly and effectively? Are links with outside agencies proving valuable and is staff training useful and relevant? Does the policy satisfy external monitoring agencies such as Ofsted? What more information would staff like? Does your practice reflect the critical success factors and fulfil the requirements of the *Code*? Does it reflect what you as a setting need? Is it reflected in other policies – for example, your equal opportunities policy on play, and so on. At the end of the day the most important aspect is the effect on the children – does the policy ensure that the children being supported are part of the setting rather than simply special?

Conclusion

Policy development and implementation cannot be adequately understood as a simple linear process whereby policy emanates from the top of a hierarchy and is implemented in a systematic way. Undoubtedly, what is stated or even intended at one end of the chain does not automatically equate with messages received at the other end. Policy embodies certain values, systems, procedures and processes which influence practice. These may ultimately define the identities and experiences of certain groups of children. Through a series of subtle processes, the policies and procedures that are ostensibly intended to promote inclusion may actually mask an exclusive philosophy. The bottom line is that all policies are 'implemented by individuals and those individuals will interpret them in their own idiosyncratic ways' (Goacher *et al.* 1988: 19). Ultimately, therefore, the success of any policy will depend on the commitment of those implementing it. This can only happen if they feel the policy will help them, if they are supported in operating the policy, if they understand the need for the policy and its contribution to effective practice, if they feel valued and enabled and they have an opportunity to identify their own training needs (Panter 1995). For policies to be inclusive, early years workers need to look at access, participation and activities. The aim is to ensure that the types of experience available to the majority of children are available to children with SEN or disabilities.

Policy development can easily be dominated by procedures and technical solutions rather than concerned with meanings and values. Those working with young children can be, and should be, instrumental in challenging the attitudes and assumptions underlying policy and practice in the early years – attitudes which may ultimately determine children's experiences, not only in the early years but for the rest of their lives.

There follows a sample policy which it is hoped will be helpful in constructing your own.

Pathfinders Day Nurseries Inclusion and Special Educational Needs Policy

1 Basic information

Aims, principles and objectives

Pathfinders aims to include children with disabilities and/or SEN, in line with the DfES *Code of Practice* 2001 and other legislation. We work closely with parents and other agencies to ensure children's individual needs are identified and met within a caring inclusive environment. Pathfinders recognizes the right of all children to be equally valued and to participate fully in the life of the nurseries and the before or after school clubs with appropriate support. We adopt a whole-setting approach which recognizes that all staff are responsible for meeting the needs of children with SEN. Our objectives are:

- to successfully implement the principles, procedures and practices recommended in the *Code of Practice*;
- to remove barriers to learning and ensure equality of opportunity for children with SEN;
- to guide, inform and support staff and parents on issues relating to SEN;

- to ensure implementation of local guidelines on SEN and inclusion;
- to meet the needs of all children identified as having SEN, ensuring progress in learning and development.

The role of the SENCO

Each nursery has an appointed SENCO who will take the lead in supporting and advising colleagues, liaising with parents, liaising with outside agencies and generally monitoring the day-to-day provision for children identified as not making adequate progress. SENCOs observe and assess children causing concern and draw up IEPs in consultation with parents, children and colleagues. They attend local authority training and maintain children's records and a register of children with SEN. The SENCO ensures that Mrs Smith, the nursery owner, is aware of any children causing concern. The schools also have SENCOs who will give advice to the nursery SENCO if necessary and the local authority has a SEN support teacher or area SENCO.

Admission arrangements

All children should be admitted regardless of SEN or disability. However, where a child has severe or complex needs, Mrs Smith should be consulted so appropriate support arrangements can be made to include the child. Children should be settled in gradually to the setting and parents informed at the outset of how we can cater for the child's needs.

Specialist facilities or staffing

Mrs Smith, the owner of Pathfinders, has a vast range of knowledge and experience in the field. Sarah Collins has completed a sign language course. Various staff across the nurseries have specific knowledge which can be drawn upon. Balsall Common, Henley and Stockingford have disabled ramps and toilets. Warwick and Cubbington are accessible although access to the toilets may need to be considered.

Arrangements for considering complaints about SEN provision

In the event of a parent expressing a concern about SEN provision staff make written notes of the cause for concern and inform the office. Staff ask the parents to contact Mrs Smith or vice versa. The normal parental complaints procedure will then be put into operation with the exception that a meeting will be arranged immediately. Support will be sought from our local area SENCO.

2 Information about policy for identification, assessment and provision

Identification and assessment arrangements for children with SEN

Initial concerns (formerly stage 1)

Where a child's learning, communication, behaviour or development is observed to be a cause for concern, staff should informally monitor and observe the child at play, noting strengths and significant areas of difficulty. An initial concerns form should be completed by the SENCO and filed. Formative assessments should be collected and filed. The SENCO should gather information from the parents. The SENCO should consider the available information and observations. If staff agree there is a cause for concern the SENCO should chat informally to the child's parents and if they agree, intervention can be planned to help the child. This is recorded on the IEP.

The setting now implements a stage of assessment and provision known as **Early Years Action** (see below). Where possible the child is consulted about his or her likes and dislikes, strengths and weaknesses using child-friendly language. The child's name is recorded on the list at the front of the **learning support file**.

Record keeping

It is essential to observe and record children and keep good records of assessments and progress. All records for children with SEN should be kept in a **learning support file**. An SEN register should be kept in the file on the pro forma provided. The following records should be kept for each child:

- initial concerns form;
- IEPs should record strategies *additional to or different from* normal arrangements for other children;
- review notes;
- observations and assessments;
- parent profiles;
- reports;
- documentation relating to outside agencies;
- correspondence with parents;

- consent forms;
- any other information relating to the child's needs or condition.

Contact details and documentation relating to external support agencies should also be kept in the file.

IEP planning and review

Early Years Action (formerly stages 1/2)

Pathfinders uses a pro forma IEP. The SENCO in discussion with staff and parents sets two or three realistic targets based on those which are going to help the child the most. Mrs Smith will help you in devising the IEP on request. The IEP should record individual targets, strategies and success criteria; who is involved, frequency of planned intervention and a date for review. IEPs should be reviewed half-termly.

Early Years Action Plus (formerly stage 3)

This is triggered when, in spite of differentiated teaching strategies and support within our normal resources, and having reviewed action taken, the child is still considered not to be making adequate progress. Parents must be notified again verbally by the SENCO and *in writing from the office* that support is going to be called in from external specialists. The request for guidance forms must be completed and sent to the office for posting with a covering letter to the parent. A member of the local support service will make an appointment and come in to observe the child. She or he will support the SENCO in further assessments and devise new targets. A new IEP will be drawn up and reviewed. If after two review periods the child is still not making adequate progress, stage 4 will be initiated on the advice of the external SEN teacher. Forms relating to this stage should be passed to the office for completion.

Request for statutory assessment (stage 4)

The specialist will be involved in the reviews and advise as to whether a request for statutory assessment is needed. If the child is still not making adequate progress on educational psychologist may come in and observe. The external agency will then help us follow the procedures for requesting statutory assessment.

Written statement (stage 5)

If it is decided by a multidisciplinary team that the child need extra support over and above provision available, a statement of SEN will be written detailing the necessary arrangements.

Allocation of resources to children with SEN

The nurseries will allocate a key worker to any child on Early Years Action or Early Years Action Plus. Special resources can be borrowed from local resource centres and toy libraries. Parents can be encouraged to bring in any special resources they use at home. Normal equipment ordering takes account of catering for children with SEN. The office has contacts and catalogues with resources which will be ordered on request.

Arrangements for providing access to the foundation stage curriculum

Taking into account health and safety, children will be given access to the full range of activities with the necessary resources, adaptations, support or equipment.

Information about staffing policies and partnerships with external agencies

SEN in-service training takes place for all staff at the staff training sessions. Information about external agencies is held at the office. Each nursery should also have the details in their SEN file. Please contact the office for advice and support. Support can be sought via the office from PLA, Kids Club Network and local authority support services.

Partnership with parents and other settings

This is considered vital at all stages of the process. Parents should be listened to and their views taken into account. Information should be shared sensitively. If a parent is having difficulty understanding or accepting their child's SEN please contact Mrs Smith and she will arrange to meet them. Outside support agencies will also speak to parents and a parent partnership scheme is available. For specific difficulties information leaflets are stored at the office. See also the partnership with parents policy. When children start school we liaise with the reception teachers via meetings and with parents consent we will pass on any relevant records. Reception teachers are welcome to observe children with SEN in the nursery before starting school.

Criteria for evaluating the success of the policy

- Have the aims been achieved?
- Are staff and parents informed, involved and clear about their role and responsibilities?
- Does the IEP planning and review process work effectively?
- Is staff training effective?
- Are positive relationships established with outside agencies?

This policy applies to all Pathfinders provision. Any questions relating to the SEN policy and procedures should be directed to Mrs Smith. The policy will be implemented from January 2003, reviewed in September 2003 and annually thereafter.

5

The changing role of the special educational needs coordinator

> This person will carry great responsibilities as well as a greatly increased workload ... who would consent to undertake this role? And how many will be able to fulfil the role adequately, without the training, resources and time needed to do the job properly?
>
> (Simmons 1994: 56–7)

This chapter examines the changing role of the special educational needs coordinator (SENCO), highlighting the numerous challenges facing SENCOs in schools and early education settings. In schools, the role has evolved from that of the traditional 'remedial teacher' to a much broader supporting role. In early education settings outside the maintained sector, the role of SENCO is more recently established. The chapter begins with a general overview of the role and responsibilities of SENCOs and looks in detail at the key features of the role. Using the perceptions and experiences of SENCOs in studies carried out after the original *Code* (DFE 1994), it then moves on to explore the problematic nature of the role and relates this to the early years context. The final section provides an overview of the knowledge and skills required to manage the role effectively and concludes by suggesting how the role can be managed in an inclusive learning environment.

The new *Code of Practice* (DfES 2001a: 1.29) makes the important point that 'provision for children with special educational needs is a matter for everyone in the setting'. In addition to the headteacher or manager, all other members of staff have important responsibilities. In practice it is the individual school or setting which can decide how to share day-to-day tasks and this will vary according to context. While the overall responsibility for implementing the *Code of Practice* lies with the setting's management group or head of setting, or in the case of schools with the governors and headteacher, the *Code* states that every setting or school should appoint a member of staff to assume responsibility for the day-to-day management of the provision for children with SEN. In non-maintained settings this may be the head of the setting. In the case of approved childminder networks the SENCO role may be shared between individual childminders or assumed by the coordinator of the network. Local early years development and childcare partnerships (EYDCPs) may also appoint 'area SENCOs' to support individual settings in fulfilling their responsibilities. In LEA-maintained nursery schools, the SENCO role is expected to be similar to that in the primary phase.

Prior to the *Code of Practice* (DfE 1994), approximately 77 per cent of schools already had a member of staff taking responsibility for SEN provision (Lewis *et al.* 1996). However, the *Code* highlighted the importance of the role and put the SENCO at the cutting edge of policy and practice. Although the revised *Code* (DfES 2001a) makes the point about the need for sharing responsibilities and allowing time for SEN coordination, it retains the key features of the role and allocates several areas of responsibility to the SENCO in mainstream primary schools. These include: overseeing the day-to-day operation of the school's SEN policy; (LSAS) coordinating provision; advising class teachers; managing learning support assistants; overseeing records for all children with SEN; liaising with parents; contributing to the in-service training of staff; and liaising with external agencies.

The revised *Code* (DfES 2001a) introduced a similar level of input from SENCOs in early education settings. The role is particularly pertinent to preschool provision in that the original *Code* itself suggested that 'the earlier action is taken, the more responsive a child is likely to be' (DfE 1994: 2.16). Without question SENCOs play a pivotal role in the early identification and assessment of children perceived as having SEN. The revised *Code* confirms the early years SENCO as a person with key responsibilities and provides a separate list of responsibilities for early years settings outside the LEA-maintained sector in receipt of government funding to provide early education places. In these settings the SENCO should have responsibility for:

- ensuring liaison with parents and other professionals;
- advising and supporting practitioners in the setting;

- ensuring appropriate IEPs are in place;
- ensuring relevant information about children with SEN is collected, recorded and updated (DfES 2001a: 34).

Warwickshire County Council's (WCC 2001) guidance for early education and childcare settings translates this into practice, stating that:

> Each early education setting will need to identify a member of staff to act as the special educational needs co-ordinator or SENCO. This member of staff will be familiar with the *Code of Practice* and will lead and co-ordinate the staff in implementing the *Code* in the setting. The SENCO will be responsible for the following aspects of SEN in practice.

It then provides a list of key responsibilities:

1 To manage the operation of the SEN policy and procedures in the setting.
2 To provide support so that all staff are informed and involved in SEN provision.
3 To liaise with parents of children with SEN and establish effective partnerships.
4 To ensure relevant background information about individual children with SEN is collected, recorded and updated.
5 To ensure that appropriate IEPs are in place and manage a cycle of IEP planning and review in accordance with the policy in the setting.
6 To liaise with all external agencies who may be involved with a child.
7 To set up and maintain a SEN register.
8 To contribute to the in-service training of staff.
9 To keep up to date with local and national changes in SEN practice and provision and keep all staff informed.
10 To monitor and review the SEN policy and practice in the setting.

(WCC 2001: 6)

This somewhat daunting list of responsibilities can be divided into four areas. First, the SENCO is an administrator of the SEN assessment policy and procedures in the setting. He or she needs to plan, maintain, review and evaluate systems and policies relating to identification, assessment and provision for children with SEN. The day-to-day administrative tasks may include photocopying IEPs, making phone calls, filing, writing letters and record keeping. SENCOs need to ensure appropriate records are kept at Early Years Action and Early Years Action Plus as well as for those children with statements.

Second, SENCOs are the link between the setting, parents and external agencies. In this capacity they would be gathering information, talking to staff, parents and children, and chairing review meetings. They would be constantly monitoring, reviewing and evaluating children's progress in order to share information with parents and external agencies.

Third, the SENCO is expected to assume a leadership and management role, acting as a consultant to colleagues. Referring to primary school SENCOs, Moss (1996) pointed out that a large part of the role involves trying to ensure that colleagues do their bit in assessing and making provision for all the children with SEN. A fundamental task for the early years SENCO is to support, guide and motivate early years workers, particularly in disseminating examples of effective practice. The role of all early years practitioners in identifying and assessing children perceived as having SEN is closely linked with the SENCO role, as they should be working together to address individual children's needs. It is the nursery workers who have close contact with the child all day, every day. In early years settings the SENCO may, for example, be expected to plan and deliver professional development to others, prepare for and manage documents for inspections (including the SEN policy, the SEN register, information given to all parents on SEN provision and evidence of training and staff development relating to SEN). She or he may also be asked to manage material resources and finance.

Fourth, the SENCO is assumed to be an expert in SEN practice and provision, directing the strategic development of teaching and learning. He or she is expected to coordinate assessment, provision and support for individual children with SEN, ensuring any child causing concern is followed though in terms of the *Code*. The SENCO should take the lead in further assessment of the child's needs, looking at both strengths and weaknesses. The SENCO should make sure that the child's IEP is appropriate in terms of targets and strategies.

The *Code* promotes the SENCO to become a key decision maker in the identification and assessment of young children perceived as having SEN. He or she is regarded as an important part of the early education settings management structure and organization. At the same time however, the emphasis on bureaucratic procedures creates the danger of reducing the SENCO role to little more than a 'things to do list'. The *Code* may be interpreted as a job description rather than a set of principles and procedures intended to improve educational provision for children with perceived SEN or a mechanism for promoting a change in professional perceptions. On the one hand, the *Code of Practice* guidance is to be welcomed as it provides a common framework and gives clarity to the role of SENCO in early education settings. On the other hand, it creates extra workload and a burden of administrative procedures. Several studies of the SENCO role following the original *Code of Practice* (DfE 1994) concluded that the increased levels of responsibility for decision making, record keeping, passing on information, organizing teams and liaising with external agencies proved difficult if not impossible (Lewis *et al.* 1996; Crowther *et al.* 1997; Jones 2000). Most of the difficulties related to lack of time to carry out the required tasks. Unless careful thought is given to these problems by headteachers, early education setting managers and childminder network coordinators, the early years, nursery and primary school SENCO roles as designated in the revised *Code* will encounter the same difficulties. A closer look at the challenge of time management following the 1994 *Code* reveals that beneath the surface of the rhetoric the SENCO role poses a number of challenges in the early years.

Managing time

Lack of time to fulfil the requirements of the original *Code* has been highlighted as a continuous and overriding issue. A survey carried out six months after the introduction of the *Code*, incorporating over 1500 primary school SENCOs, reported incredible amounts of paperwork, lack of time to review the IEPs with other staff, lack of time to liaise with parents and outside agencies and bureaucratic dimensions of the *Code* as being the major challenges. One SENCO referred to 'Thirty-two hours of extra paperwork during the Christmas holiday'(Lewis *et al.* 1996: 38). These findings were reiterated in a study by a team from the University of Newcastle (Crowther *et al.* 1997) which carried out a survey across seven LEAs and 67 school visits. The study found that many SENCOs felt challenged by the administrative aspects of SEN provision. As well as time for paperwork, the SENCOs were struggling to find time to arrange and attend meetings with parents, class teachers and outside agencies. The SENCOs appeared to be juggling between meeting the needs of the children and colleagues and fulfilling the requirements of the *Code*. Indeed, the primary SENCOs had the equivalent of less than half a minute per child per week (Lewis *et al.* 1996). As the following quotations show, SENCOs felt as though they were on a continuous carousel, constantly stopping and starting again:

SENCO is an M25 job, going round in congested circles.

(Lewis *et al.* 1996: 37)

The work is never done and there is never an end to it. You just get all your work done, all your reviews done, all IEPs written and you are really working up to it and you see progress. Then you think, I've got to stop and interrupt all this, because it's review time and I've got to meet all these people again.

(Jones 2000)

Although the *Code* recommends that SENCOs should liaise extensively with colleagues, non-contact time in primary schools and early education settings is severely limited. The University of Newcastle survey concluded that 40 per cent of SENCOs in primary schools had no timetabled time for SEN work and almost 70 per cent had half a day a week or less (Crowther *et al.* 1997). Other studies found that almost 70 per cent of primary SENCOs thought their non-contact time was completely or fairly inadequate, mainly due to lack of finance (Lewis *et al.* 1996). A later study (Jones 2000) found that instead of having dedicated 'talk time', much of the conversation in the staff rooms during breaktimes and lunchtimes revolves around children with 'problems'. The situation is typical in may preschool settings and is far from ideal. Jones (2000) quotes one SENCO, who explained:

They snatch me whenever they see me. Sometimes it's at very inappropriate times. When really we should sit down somewhere quiet but I haven't got an office. It's very open and that's a real problem. I've got information that I'm working with on the computer screen, which shouldn't really be seen. And when people really want to see me they sometimes just stop me in the corridor which is just inappropriate you know. And we can be overheard.

Both the content and the delivery of this next quote convey the degree of frustration and confusion:

I just feel that the time ... limitation is actually spoiling what is a very nice job. Because I'm constantly feeling I'm not ... I'm not fulfilling what I want to fulfil, what I ought to be doing. It's ... it's a bit of a nag really and particularly when I'm spending so much extra time. I mean the time, the time that I spend you know, preparing and doing all the paperwork that goes with it. It just adds up to so many hours. But as it is when I know that I could be brought to task and be told that I am not fulfilling what I should be doing. Then I feel that it's ... although there are children in the infants who need my help and I suppose under the *Code of Practice* ought to have it. I could be in trouble if they don't get it. I've spoken to the head and she said that there just isn't any way that I can do the job and make it worthwhile at all if I spread myself any thinner.

The situation is exacerbated in Key Stage 1 and LEA nurseries attached to schools as the SENCO in a primary school may also have other responsibilities and be a full-time class teacher. Crowther *et al.* (1997: 49) found that over 90 per cent of primary SENCOs had other responsibilities, citing one teacher who said, 'Wearing too many hats makes me less concentrated on SENCO work and organization'. In an early education setting the majority of SENCOs are almost certain to be people working with the children on a day-to-day basis.

The SENCO Guide (DfEE 1997b) suggests that even in small schools the SENCO role can be time-consuming and demanding. Presumably the same point can be made about early education settings outside the maintained sector. It cannot be assumed that the numbers of children in early education settings are automatically considerably fewer than in a primary school. Given that up to one-fifth of the children may be on the setting's SEN register and taking into account that settings with part-time attendance, for example, registered for 30 children may in fact have 60 or 70 children throughout the course of a week, some early education settings have as many children with SEN to oversee as some primary schools. Therefore, the role of the SENCO may be equally taxing. SENCOs in early education are also less likely to be qualified teachers, work in a climate of tighter financial constraints and with staff who have little or no non-contact time or time set aside for staff training.

It is hardly surprising, therefore, that the revised *Code* (DfES 2001a: 4.17) makes the point that in early education settings the SENCO will require sufficient time to undertake their responsibilities and suggests settings 'may find it effective for the SENCO to be a member of the senior management team'. Undoubtedly, the setting manager must allow the SENCO dedicated time to carry out his or her duties. Time allocated should be in proportion to the number of children on the SEN register. It might also be useful to share some of the tasks with colleagues. Apart from the time management issue, the paperwork involved in administering the *Code of Practice* may be a source of anxiety for early education setting SENCOs, particularly in the early stages. Studies of schools after the introduction of the original *Code* in 1994 certainly found this to be the case.

Managing paperwork

'The CoP [*Code of Practice*] is a vast administration edifice which inhibits the good practice established since Warnock. It forces SENCOs into extra secretarial duties' (Lewis *et al.* 1996. 38). SENCOs interviewed by Jones (2000) about the nature of their role again repeatedly returned to the theme of manageability. It appeared that the SENCO was expected to shoulder much of the responsibility for implementing the *Code's* recommendations. The comments from the SENCOs below summarize a general consensus that the paperwork was unmanageable, especially writing the IEPs, and they were convinced that the *Code* would be impracticable in the longer term:

> It's not workable. I can't … I can't imagine that this level of input into special needs can be continued.

> It's fairly unwieldy really. I think it's just impractical. Well, I found that it made the job much less teaching and much more paperwork. I didn't realize the job really entailed writing up all this paperwork.

Most practitioners appreciated that accurate and meaningful record keeping was a crucial part of the assessment procedure. However, the problem in schools and early education settings is finding a balance between amassing enough detail to be sufficient for a referral at a later stage, and short enough to be practical and not too time-consuming. A headteacher makes the point:

> One of the problems … but sometimes it's a double-edged sword isn't it? It's the enormous amount of paperwork that is generated through the *Code* with the individual IEPs. Now we know they have to be done from a child's point of view, I'm sure that being very focused on two or three very small structured steps that you're expecting them to have taken has enormous advantages. But if you're in a school such as this, where quite a number of children will be on the *Code*, you're looking at an enormous workload both for the class teacher and for the SENCO.

This comment illustrates that while schools are aware of the potential educational benefits of the *Code*, these may be being undermined by the workload issues, particularly in schools where a high number of children are on the SEN register. When the above interview took place, the situation was made even more difficult as the SENCOs were obliged to pass on copies of the IEPs to those involved with the children on the SEN register: for example the LSA, the class teacher and the educational psychologist. During her time in schools, Jones (2000) found that in one 6-year-old child's file alone there were 150 sheets of paper. Approximately half of these were generated by outside agencies. SENCOs found this aspect of the role tedious and frustrating:

> I felt that I was a very highly paid photocopying person, because I spent an awful lot of time photocopying bits of paper for the class teacher, for the child's file and for the educational psychologist file. I felt I spent an awful lot of time doing that type of thing but I don't enjoy that at all.

This SENCO clearly attached little value to the content of the IEPs or other 'bits of paper'. The IEPs were not viewed as working educational planning tools but merely as a record-keeping exercise. The implicit assumption was that the educational psychologist would merely file the information, rather than use it for any valuable purpose. The interviewee indicates a sense of low job satisfaction and frustration at the time-consuming nature of the photocopying. She felt that the qualified teaching job she was being paid for had been reduced to that of a 'photocopying person'.

The point that the paperwork was little more than an annoying nuisance was also emphasized by a headteacher at one school. Having been acting SENCO for a few weeks, he felt that not only was the paperwork a waste of a teacher's valuable time, but also that the meetings and reviews were sometimes fruitless:

> The initial role is one really of overseeing the *Code of Practice* put into place. And now the teacher is spending most of her time pushing pieces of paper around and going to meetings and it is annoying, it is frustrating and some of the meetings are meetings to discuss the next meeting.

In order to manage the role effectively the SENCO needs to develop particular expertise, knowledge, skills and attributes. As a starting point each SENCO should carry out a personal audit in order to assess his or her own development needs. The Teacher Training Agency's (TTA) *National Standards for Special Educational Needs Coordinators* (1998) set out some suggested additional knowledge, skills, attributes and expertise required by those coordinating provision in schools. These have been adapted below to apply to early education settings.

SENCOs should have knowledge and understanding of:

- the characteristics of effective teaching and learning strategies and how they can support children with SEN and improve or maintain children's learning, behaviour and development;

- how to devise and evaluate systems for identifying, assessing and reviewing children's learning and developmental needs;
- the nature and purpose of IEPs, how they are formulated and how they can be used to best effect;
- how information ICT can be used to help children gain access to the curriculum, learn and communicate;
- up-to-date, relevant legislation, research and inspection evidence;
- the requirements to communicate information to LEAs, external agencies, parents and other schools or settings;
- the scope and role of local support services including voluntary schemes;
- the range of ways available for working in partnership with parents;
- how to contribute to professional development of other staff.

(Adapted from TTA 1998: 8)

SENCOs should possess the following skills and attributes. Leadership and decision-making skills in order to:

- create and foster confidence and commitment among staff to meet the needs of all children;
- set standards and provide examples of good practice in identifying, assessing and meeting children's SEN;
- provide professional direction to the work of others;
- develop policy, record systems and procedures;
- manage resources;
- make decisions based on information/evidence;
- judge when there is a need to consult outside agencies.

Communication and self-management skills in order to:

- communicate effectively orally and in writing with children, collea-gues, parents and external agencies;
- negotiate and consult with parents and outside agencies;
- chair reviews, case conferences and meetings effectively;
- prioritize and manage own time;
- take responsibility for own professional development.

(Adapted from TTA 1998: 9–10)

As with any leadership and management role, personal qualities are a key factor of the SENCO role. The SENCO should have a personal impact on the setting, demonstrating enthusiasm and commitment, self-con-fidence, reliability and integrity as well as intellectual ability and the ability to be adaptable to a variety of situations. Where there is no single individual with the knowledge, skills and attributes you could consider dividing the responsibilities between two or more early years workers. A nursery assistant, for example, could handle the one-to-one support in enabling children to achieve the IEP targets and be responsible for the record keeping. The head of the setting could liaise with the external agencies and write the SEN policy. An officer in charge could be responsible for sharing information with parents. As well as identifying his or her own professional development needs the SENCO needs to find out what help and advice their colleagues need. As a starting point for discussion, setting staff could also be asked to complete a simple summary of their needs for advice. They could be asked to complete a simple questionnaire (see Table 5.1) and reflect on their skills and knowledge in meeting the demands of working with children who have SEN.

Table 5.1 Questionnaire evaluating staff development needs

How confident are you in the following areas?	Totally	Fairly	More information and/or training required
How to identify children with SEN and assess their needs			
How IEPs are formulated including setting targets			
How to monitor, review and record the progress of pupils with SEN at Early Years Action			
Strategies for working with children who have: • learning difficulties • communication difficulties • emotional and behaviour difficulties			
How to monitor, review and record the progress of pupils with SEN at Early Years Action Plus			
Write your strengths and expertise here			
Add your personal needs and other comments here			

Towards effective practice

The *Code* brings status and clarity to the early years SENCO role. However, in order to be effective in their role SENCOs in early education settings should be enabled to exploit the potential educational benefits of the *Code* while minimizing bureaucratic demands. This can be done by ensuring adequate resourcing and support are provided, including clerical support and access to ICT. A major focus of the role is to convince colleagues that SEN is everyone's responsibility not just that of the SENCO. Therefore it is essential that the early years SENCO is given the opportunity to disseminate the underlying principles of the *Code* as well as the mechanics of carrying out the procedures. Where the whole school or early education setting is committed to the SEN policy it is more likely to be effective and the importance of spending time with colleagues cannot be overemphasized. The whole-school/setting approach will enable provision for children with SEN to be viewed as an integral rather than distinct part of the setting's educational provision. All early years workers need to regard the *Code* as a flexible guide to improving the educational provision for children perceived as having SEN and not interpret it literally as a set of burdensome and bureaucratic rules to be followed. Clear lines of communication and systematic procedures need to be developed.

Use should be made of the local area's SENCOs and outside agencies for advice on policy, practice or about a child's learning or behaviour at Early Years Action Plus (and earlier if necessary). The new role of area SENCO is becoming increasingly important. They can help in a number of areas including:

- assessing and observing children;
- strategies for managing learning and behaviour;
- help with IEPs and reviews;
- information for parents;
- information on local training and support services;
- resources;
- writing policies.

Effective SEN coordination will lead to a reduction of barriers to learning and a number of other key outcomes.

Key outcomes of SEN coordination

The role of SENCO may be problematic in a practical sense, yet it offers unique opportunities to develop relationships with a wide range of adults and children. Once the role moves beyond the paperwork to a more collaborative, interactive and dynamic role, practice will be more effective. There are a number of ways the SENCO can continue to influence teaching and learning. The key outcomes of SEN coordination are:

- children who make progress towards targets established in IEPs are helped to access the foundation stage curriculum;
- children who are motivated to learn and develop self-esteem and confidence as young learners;
- staff who are familiar with the setting policy and its philosophy towards meeting the needs of all children;
- staff who are able to identify children who may need extra support;
- staff who can communicate with the SENCO and who have high expectations of all children;
- parents who understand the setting's approaches to inclusion, who have targets set for their children and who feel fully involved at each stage in the graduated assessment procedure;
- setting managers who recognize the importance of a relevant and developmentally appropriate curriculum, reflect inclusion in all policies and support the SENCO in their duties;
- management committees who understand the role of the setting in relation to the children with SEN and receive regular updates on policy;
- outside agencies who receive accurate information and spend time in the setting effectively (TTA 1998).

Conclusion

Although the work of SENCOs will vary according to context, a number of conclusions can be drawn from this review of the SENCO's role. The role of the SENCO is complex and changing. It will continue to change in response to the needs of children and staff and this is likely to take years rather than months. The *Code* (DfES 2001a) and its predecessor promote the SENCO to become a key decision maker in the identification and assessment of young children perceived as having SEN. He or she is to be regarded as an important and integral part of a setting's management structure and organization. At the same time, however, the emphasis on bureaucratic procedures inhibits effective practice. Without time, training or resources it will be difficult to carry out the role effectively. As a result, the *Code* may continue to be interpreted as a set of bureaucratic procedures rather than a set of principles and practices intended to improve provision for children with perceived SEN. If the SENCO is not able to function effectively, the whole-school or setting approach cannot be advocated. Conversely, without the whole-school or setting approach the SENCO cannot function effectively.

The role of the SENCO can potentially be marginalized and stressful. SENCOs will be trying to meet the needs of a whole range of people – children, parents, colleagues, outside agencies. At the same time they will be coping with increased administrative demands, and trying to satisfy local and national pressures to meet the demands of legislation. Meeting individual educational needs must be an integral part of the planning, teaching and assessment cycle for all children. The role of the SENCO is pivotal in promoting strategies for effective learning in early childhood and in supporting inclusion in the early years for the benefit of all young children, not only those perceived as having SEN. Although personalities, organization, status and resources all have a part to play, it is the setting's philosophy that is most influential. It is the philosophy that underpins policy and practice and provides the impetus and direction to help staff move forward in their thinking and promote common goals (Pickup 1995).

6

Parents, children and professionals working together

All parents of children with special educational needs should be treated as partners.

(DfES 2001a: 2.2)

The rhetoric of parent partnership currently permeates almost every aspect of educational practice. Parental involvement, responsibility and inclusion in both decision making and service delivery are integral parts of all the legislation and guidance on SEN. However, the term 'partnership' can be vague and misleading and is open to a number of interpretations in theory and practice. This chapter explores the development of the notion of 'partnership with parents', now a well-rehearsed phrase in early education settings and schools. The first section looks at the background and rationale for involving parents in their children's learning and development. The second section focuses on the range of definitions and models of parent partnership which have evolved over time. The final section draws on the *Code of Practice* (DfES 2001a) and case studies to translate the rhetoric of partnership into practice. It makes the point that in an inclusive early education setting, partnership is not only concerned with working with parents but also with ascertaining the views of the child.

According to the Children Act (1989) a parent is the person who has 'parental responsibility' for the care and upbringing of children born to them or adopted by them. The child will generally be living with them and the parent has full legal responsibility for the child's care and upbringing until legally defined adulthood or the age of 16. Parents of children over compulsory school age have a legal duty to make sure that their children receive an efficient full-time education suitable to any SEN they may have (Education Act 1996: Section 7).

Historically, all parents, not just those of children with SEN, were considered to be external to the efficient education of children in schools. Often they were not allowed in without appointments and were considered little more than a tiresome nuisance. They were expected to send their children to school and make an occasional appearance at the school play or sports day. In spite of the fact that over 75 children in the UK are born or diagnosed every day with a serious disability or rare syndrome, until the 1970s the usual experience of parents of children born or identified as having a handicap or disability was little or no support at all. They were told the 'diagnosis' by a doctor and left to cope as best they could (Buckley 1994).

However, there has been a significant shift towards encouraging parents of children, with and without SEN, to be involved with and informed about their children's education. The potential benefits of joint efforts between parents and professionals to enhance learning and development has been repeatedly sanctioned in successive legislation and official documents since the late 1960s. The Plowden Report (1967) suggested that a close partnership between parents and professionals is essential and the Taylor Report (Taylor 1977) spelt out the rights of parents to have a say in the running of their child's school and to be informed about what is happening in the school. In relation to children with SEN the Warnock Report (DES 1978) heralded a new approach which regarded parents as equal partners in the educational process. Warnock (DES 1978: 150) subscribed to a philosophy of parents 'rather than teachers' as the 'main educators' of their children, stating unequivocally that 'it is an essential part of our thesis that parents must be advised, encouraged and supported so that they can in turn effectively help their children' and recommending that 'reinforcement and skilled support should be provided for parents of children with disabilities or significant difficulties in their earliest years' (DES 1978: 5.31). The Education Act (1981) gave parents the right to be consulted on matters relating to the assessment and placement of children with SEN. This profound shift towards acceptance that parents can play an active part in children's learning has been enshrined in the notion of 'partnership with parents'. Nevertheless, reflecting on the chapter in the Warnock Report entitled 'Parents as Partners', Mary Warnock (1985: 12) acknowledges that the idea of equal partnership may have been rather ambitious: 'I think, looking back, we exaggerated. In educational matters, parents cannot be equals to teachers if teachers are to be regarded as true professionals ... parents should realise that they cannot have the last word. It is a question of collaboration not partnership.' Hegarty (1993) supports this view and suggests that the concept of equal partners espoused in Warnock is not particularly helpful as it can 'smack of empty rhetoric and be misleading in practice' (p. 155). Instead he proposes five dimensions of collaboration focused on information, curriculum, behaviour problems, personal support and liaison with professionals, and points out that while it is feasible to envisage equality, sometimes it is neither helpful nor necessary in practice.

Defining partnership

The word 'partnership' is used to describe the relationship between parents and professionals, including teachers and early years practitioners. Central to the notion of partnership is that we should not only listen to parents' views but also value them. Some writers refer to 'complementary expertise' (Davis 1985) in that the expertise of the parent complements that of the professional. Others refer to 'equivalent expertise' (Wolfendale 1983) where parents are viewed as having equal strengths. Mittler and Mittler (1994) also suggest that partnership involves a full sharing of knowledge, skills and experiences and must be equal. However, it has been argued that partnership is not easy to bring about (Wolfendale 1992; Gascoigne 1995; Dale 1996). This may be because the partnership relationship is unproductive if it does not lead to empowerment of the parent. In other words, the parent should have 'full and equal rights and opportunities to participation and power-sharing in special needs processes and decision making' (Wolfendale 1997: 4).

The reasons for working in partnership with parents of children with SEN are no different from those advanced for working with parents of all young children. Ongoing parental involvement from an early age ensures not only mutual trust, but also the benefits of implementing decisions made jointly about children in the home. Pound (1999) suggests that partnership with parents of all young children and those who work with them in early years settings is not something to be to considered negotiable; instead she views it as absolutely essential. In relation to children with SEN, if one accepts that special needs can only be meaningfully interpreted in the context of children's total lives, then parents are a crucial component in ensuring educational and social success. The *Code of Practice* (DfE 1994: 2.28) points out that help given by professionals will not be wholly effective unless it builds upon parents' capacity to be involved, or unless parents 'feel that the professionals have taken account of what they say and treat their views and anxieties as intrinsically important'. Dale (1996: 24) makes a strong case for parental involvement, citing a host of reasons for professionals to work in partnership with parents:

- the professional needs parental cooperation to do their own job effectively;
- parents are a potential resource for helping their child with SEN;
- parents need support and guidance to help them carry out their parenting role;
- lack of professional support can have a disabling effect on parents;
- the family has a key role to play in the child's life;
- children are individuals with their own wishes and feelings and the family has unique knowledge of child;
- families provide continuity throughout childhood;
- children's needs cannot be separated from interactions within the family context;
- parents want to be more involved in activities and decisions on their children's education and childcare.

The *Code of Practice* (DfES 2001a: 2.2) also acknowledges that 'Parents hold key information and have a critical role to play in their children's education. They have unique strengths, knowledge and experience to contribute to the shared view of a child's needs and the best ways of supporting them'. Clearly, there is no shortage of official support for the view that parents should be involved in the educational process. However, official pronouncements do not automatically result in a change of attitudes and practices. The way parents are involved in their children's education and care varies greatly between settings. As Wolfendale (1997: 1–2) reminds us, 'Partnership is far from achieved for many parents: too many parents remain unreached and seemingly, unreachable ... the power balance is unevenly weighted towards professionals'.

Partnership in practice

Several proposed models of parent/professional relationships have evolved over time. Cunningham and Davis (1985), for example, looked at ways in which parents participated in intervention programmes and identified three distinct models of parent-professional relationships which they called the 'expert', the 'transplant' and the 'consumer' models. Appleton and Minchom (1991) developed an 'empowerment' model, while Dale (1996) introduced a model which she called the 'negotiating model'. While no single model can encompass the intricacies and complexities of real life, these models have been adapted and translated into levels of increasing involvement and empowerment for parents in early years settings. Viewed in this way they provide a useful starting point for discussion between staff as to your current position and where you would like to be at some point in the future.

Level 0

The *obstructive model* – parents are largely unsupported and receive little or no help from professionals. In practice parents of all children, except perhaps a favoured few, wait outside locked doors and hand the child over at the nursery door. They do not enter the main play areas and are not allowed to wait a few minutes for the child to settle. No initial or home visits take place. If parents want to talk to staff they have to make an appointment at the nursery's convenience. While some parents may be treated in a friendly manner, others are viewed as a nuisance and a source of friction. Information is only imparted on a need to know basis. This approach is based on the idea that parents should be seen little and not heard at all.

Level 1

The *expert model* is exemplified by the professional taking control and making decisions and the parent being the passive recipient of services. In practice, partnership is minimal as the parents and children become increasingly dependent on professionals who think they know best. Information is given without explanation and parents are told about their child using formal language and professional jargon. The approach is insensitive and the professional shows no empathy with the parent.

Level 2

The *transplant model* of parental involvement, whereby professionals transplant or share skills and expertise with the parents, but this is still not a full partnership as the professional retains control. This model emerged in the early 1970s and is exemplified by home-visiting teachers who show parents how to teach particular skills to their child and then go away, returning the next week to show them the next step. Another example of this model is the Portage scheme, developed in Wisconsin (Shearer and Shearer 1972), a model of shared teaching, assessment and review originally conceived as a method through which parents of pre-school children could participate in the educational development of their children. At this level the parent is seen as a resource and although the parental role is valued, it is still a professionally dominated approach. This type of model may overburden the parent and could promote an unhelpful emphasis on parents absorbing 'teacher' skills instead of interacting more naturally with their child. It does not exemplify the 'equivalent expertise' suggested by Wolfendale (1989).

Level 3

The *consumer model* developed by Cunningham and Davis (1985) acknowledges that parents have considerable knowledge to be shared and have a right to make decisions regarding services. The status of parents in this model is higher. Settings operating at this level give parents rights and credit them with expertise in that they have a unique knowledge of their own child and family. Here there is a shift of power from the professional to the parent. It is the beginnings of true partner-ship, with the parent exercising some control in the provision of services for their child. It is based on a working relationship with mutual respect and a shared sense of responsibility for decision making.

Level 4

The *empowerment model* put forward by Appleton and Minchom (1991) views the family as a social network. Here the early years practitioner takes account of family needs in planning any intervention and empowers the parent to take up a position as partner. The aim at this level is to promote the parent's sense of control over decisions affecting their child and to be sensitive to the parent's choices.

Level 5

The *negotiating model* of Dale (1996) builds on previous models. As the name indicates, practitioners working with parents at this level will be focusing on negotiation as a key factor in partnership work: 'It offers a framework for exploring a partnership practice that can embody or respond to the constraints and reality of actual power relations and positions of the parent and professional within our present and future societal contexts' (Dale 1996: 14). In practice this level is characterized by two-way dialogue and 'a working relationship where the partners use negotiation and joint decision making to resolve differences of opinion and disagreement in order to reach some kind of shared perspective or jointly agreed decision on issues of mutual concern' (1996: 14). This approach promotes collaboration and shared decision making to a point where all sides are happy with the decisions. The premise is that both parent and professional have highly valuable contributions to make. Although the professional still retains powers they are considerably weaker than in earlier models.

Carpenter (1996) summarizes key lessons we can learn from these models and makes some recommendations which can be applied to the way we approach all parents, not just those whose children have SEN. He suggests parents and those working with children should be honest with and willing to learn from each other. He advises that both parties should treat each other with respect and dignity. Ideally we should all be willing to admit our mistakes and work collaboratively and cooperatively with parents. Finally, he recommends 'Be yourself' (1996: 240).

Partnership in practice

The *Code* (DfES 2001a: 2.2) sets out a number of key principles in communicating and working in partnership with parents. It makes the point that early education settings as well as schools should implement these principles. It highlights the importance of positive attitudes, user-friendly information and awareness of support needs. The principles for making communication effective are that professionals should:

- acknowledge and draw on parental expertise in relation to their child;
- focus on the child's strengths as well as areas of additional need;
- recognize the personal and emotional investment of parents and be aware of their feelings;
- ensure that parents understand procedures, are aware of how to access support and are given documents before meetings;
- respect the validity of different viewpoints and seek constructive ways of reconciling differing views;
- respect the differing needs parents themselves may have such as communication or linguistic barriers;
- recognize the need for flexibility in the timing and structure of meetings.

The *Code* suggests parents should be supported and empowered to recognize and fulfil their responsibilities as parents and play an active and valued role in their children's education. Translating these principles into practice is best viewed from three aspects – information, involvement and support.

Information and involvement

In spite of best intentions, achieving information sharing is not always easy and needs careful thought. Parents have the right to have access to information, advice and support during assessment and any decision-making processes about their child's special educational provision. Parents should have knowledge of their child's entitlement within the SEN framework and be able to make their views known about how their child is educated. The starting point for this is in developing and sharing the SEN policy and ensuring user-friendly information and procedures. Formal language may have little meaning and written information should be supplemented with oral communication. There should be regular opportunities for personal contact and the parents need to know who their first point of contact is. They need to be informed of your procedures for acting on parental concerns and be aware of how parents are actually involved in decision making. The setting should also provide parents with information on support services, including the local parent partnership service. You could use the government's guide for parents and carers (DfES 2001d) as a tool for explaining the framework to parents and give them a copy to take away alongside any local information.

According to the Education Act 1996 an LEA must arrange for the parent of any child in their area who has SEN to be provided with information about matters relating to those needs. These arrangements have been embraced in parent partnership services. Their overall aim is to provide a service which enables parents to play a more active and informed role in their child's education. It is important for all providers of childcare and education to be aware of their local parent partnership and pass on contact details to parents. Parent partnership services are a source of practical and impartial advice and offer a range of services, including putting families in touch with local support groups. Warwickshire Parent Partnership Service, for example, offers a range of support for parents and carers of children identified as having SEN including a system of voluntary independent parental supporters.

Involving parents in delivering the curriculum is prominent in home-based teaching programmes for children under 3 and can be continued by involving parents in planning, supporting and reviewing IEP targets. At Early Years Action Plus parental permission is needed and outside agencies will not become involved with a specific child without parental consent. This is much more likely to be achieved if the parents have been fully informed since the initial concern. Written information leaflets may be helpful and an opportunity to meet the person from the external agency is essential. Meetings with parents should have a structure which allows all parties to give their views. Many parents of children attending day nurseries are at work during these times, and may need to make further childcare arrangements to allow them to attend meetings at other times. Meeting times therefore need to be tailored to suit the needs of parents, particularly those with more than one child. As the following two comments from parents show, the quality of involvement is variable:

> I do not understand the system entirely and do not feel involved. I am told what is happening. It is extremely stressful. It took a long time to get the school to acknowledge my child's needs.

> I have been very pleased with all the help, support and understanding I have received.

Support and sharing concerns

Parents will need varying degrees of support and this can be offered by providing access to the setting. Flexibility is important here. A good starting point is to actually ask parents what types of support they would find helpful. Examples include home visits, drop in sessions, SEN information evenings, parent to parent support and social activities. Parents need to feel that their wishes, feelings and perspectives are considered and respected. This is particularly important at the point at which initial concerns are shared. If you know the child has SEN beforehand it is useful to arrange a home visit. This helps shift the power to the parent as they are more likely to relax in a familiar environment. It also helps you build a broader picture of the child's context.

If concerns are raised after the child starts at the early education setting, parents also need to be made aware. There is no perfect or single way to share concerns with parents. If you have identified a learning or behavioural difficulty you need to consider carefully how and when to discuss this with the parents. Will you make an appointment or will you ask to speak to them at the end of a session? Will you telephone or write? How this is worded is crucial and can vary according to the level of concern and the individual parent. First, find out if the parents themselves have any concerns or have noticed anything. If not, then you should mention your concerns. While you should be sensitive, gentle and caring you also need to be honest and open. It is important to have observed the child carefully and be certain of the evidence base of your initial concerns. You should focus on the importance of working together to optimize each individual child's progress. Allow parents time to understand what you are saying about the child's difficulties, how mild or severe they might be and what the setting is doing to address them. It is also just as important to share the child's achievements with the parents as it is to share your concerns. You can sensitively discuss any factors at home which may affect the child in the nursery. Sometimes, as shown in the case below, disclosing concerns is unproblematic, especially where relationships are already very close.

Case 1: Hannah

Hannah, aged 2, was the third child to attend the nursery and staff knew her mum well. Her mum was a teacher. Staff had noticed Hannah was slow to respond to her name and to instructions. After observing her at play they noticed she seemed to be taking cues from other children and needed gestures or physical prompts to participate. The SENCO thought perhaps it was her hearing. When her mum came to collect Hannah, she called Hannah's name. Hannah had her back to her at the time and did not respond. The SENCO said informally, 'We've been watching Hannah for a few days and we wondered if she has had her hearing checked lately as she doesn't always seem to hear.' Her mum said Hannah had failed her previous test and was due to go back. Eventually Hannah had a hearing aid.

Sometimes the process may not be so straightforward. As the two cases below show, when parents have little experience of young children they may find it hard to understand and indeed accept that their child is different in some way from children of the same age. Some parents experience guilt, grief and even shame – for example, if the concern is about behaviour they may feel you are implying it is their fault. As a result, and as shown in Case 2, they may initially be defensive. Early years workers need to accept and respect parents' response even if it is denial. It is crucial to explain that you want to put in place some help for the child and use smaller steps to help him or her progress. If, as in Case 3, the parents flatly refuse to cooperate you can continue with differentiation and low-level monitoring. However, *you cannot call on the advice of external agencies*. In cases such as this, parents could be given time and approached again at a later date.

Case 2: Ron

Ron was 4 years' old and his behaviour had been causing concern for some time. At first, staff had thought it to be immaturity. However, after observing Ron they noticed he did not play or interact with other children or adults and he was often disruptive. He said a few words but his language was stilted and it was difficult to gain eye contact with him. Staff were reluctant to speak to his dad about it as they sensed he would be unhappy. They asked the setting manager to intervene and she also observed and agreed there was cause for concern. When Ron's dad came to collect Ron she asked for a quiet word in the office. She said that Ron was well settled and liked playing outside and with the cars, but she had noticed that he didn't really play much with the other children and seemed to be a bit of a loner. She asked if he had noticed anything at home. He seemed immediately defensive and said Ron was fine at home and was always playing and talking to his cousins. The setting manager accepted this and said that they would keep an eye on him over the next two weeks and then speak again. She asked him to do the same. Two weeks later, she explained that they would like to set some targets and implement some strategies to help Ron make more friends in the nursery. The setting drew up an IEP and talked it through with Ron's dad but in spite of intensive help Ron still did not interact with the others. The SENCO wanted to call in an outside specialist and asked the father's permission. Over time, he had come to agree with the staff and gave his consent. Ron was starting school in six months' time and following several visits from a support teacher and the educational psychologist, a request for statutory assessment was put forward. The setting manager emphasized all along that the whole purpose of the action was to help Ron make progress and give him support. She also emphasized that this was normal procedure in all cases where children needed some extra input.

Case 3: Leanne

Leanne, a 3-year-old child, had very poor coordination, and she fell over frequently. She had difficulty on the slide steps and often tripped over her own feet. Her running seemed to veer to one side and she dribbled. In other aspects, such as language, she was well ahead of her peer group. Staff were concerned and pointed out to her mum that Leanne was in the accident book more times than normal and would she mind if they monitored her physical coordination closely for a couple of weeks. Her mum was not pleased and said Leanne was absolutely fine, never fell over at home and it must be because she was tired, the slide was too big, and she was not being supervised properly. The staff tried on several occasions to approach Leanne's mum, even inviting her in to observe herself for a session, but she would not be persuaded. The staff decided to observe and monitor Leanne but did not draw up a formal IEP. They intended to ask the setting manager to write a carefully worded letter to Leanne's mum confirming the nature of the concerns that had been expressed and including an open invitation for both parents to contact the nursery if they wished to discuss any aspect of Leanne's care and education. However, the parents withdrew Leanne from the setting before the letter could be sent.

In most cases parents really do appreciate it if you are open and honest, with the proviso that you are sure of the grounds for your expression of concern. Each case is different and staff should take time to establish clearly the nature of the difficulty and how it might be approached. An overview of Thomas' case illustrates a more complex and time-consuming approach but one which can reap benefits for the child, the parents and the professionals.

Case 4: Thomas

Thomas started at the nursery at 18 months. He was the only child of a young couple who were new to the area. Staff immediately noticed on his initial visit that Thomas had some unusual characteristics. He communicated by squealing, and rocked when agitated. His fingers were in the clasped position and he needed a lot of individual support to participate in activities. He loved music and smiled when spoken to but appeared to be delayed in a number of areas. Within a few days of his starting, staff pointed out their concerns to the SENCO, who was also the setting manager and had already noticed Thomas but was waiting to see if other staff would say anything. Over a four-week period the SENCO and the staff observed Thomas carefully, noting his strengths and areas of need. The SENCO then asked his mum for a quiet word and explained that the staff had been observing Thomas since he started and would like to meet with her and Thomas' father to discuss his settling in and general development. She agreed and both parents came to a meeting. They were given a cup of tea and the setting manager began to explain the concerns. She referred to Thomas' strengths, saying that he had settled in well, that he liked music and was very happy in the nursery. She then said that the normal procedure was to observe children when they first started and in Thomas' case these observations had raised a concern about his development. She stressed that it was not major but needed to be shared. She used specific examples from the observations to illustrate the concern. The parents listened carefully and said they were surprised but as it was their first child they had no one to compare him with. His grandmother had also looked after him most of the time before he came to the nursery. The SENCO suggested that, as a precaution, his mother might like to take Thomas to the GP to gain another view. He was referred to the Child Development Centre and was found to have general learning difficulties and dyspraxia. He was provided with a Portage support worker. Parents, staff and support agencies worked closely together on shared strategies and Thomas made good progress. Although at first it was a shock for the parents they became very close to the SENCO and later said how glad they were that the concerns had been voiced at an early stage.

For each of these scenarios there are hundreds of others each with their own different experiences and approaches. Hard and fast rules cannot be applied to parent partnership. It is more a matter of empathy and trust on both sides. Yet there is also a third component involved in the 'eternal triangle of intervention' (Jones 1998) – that is to say, the child.

Until recently most discussion has related to parents and professionals making decisions on the child's behalf until adulthood. Children are disadvantaged in that they are deemed to be 'too young' to have a view. Recent legislation and the recognition of children's rights have highlighted the importance of ensuring that children participate in the decision-making process. The Children Act (1989) emphasized the rights of the child to have their feelings and wishes known and taken into account when decisions are made about them. Article 12 of the UN Convention on the Rights of the Child (United Nations 1989), ratified by the UK in 1991, also states the right of the child to express an opinion in any matters or procedure affecting them and to have that opinion taken into account according to the age, maturity and capability of the child.

The involvement of children in their own assessment and review arrangements was a major innovation in the fist *Code* and was strengthened in the revised version. The SEN *Code of Practice* (DfES 2001a) emphasizes the importance of seeking and taking account of the ascertainable wishes and feelings of children and involving them when decisions are made that affect them. The *SEN Toolkit* (DfES 2001c: 1) sets out a number of principles of children's participation in decision making, the key premise being that everyone working in the school or setting is committed to ensuring the long-term involvement of pupils. Pupil participation needs to be built on a culture of listening to children from an early age. Even young children can be helped to comment on their feelings, wishes and experiences using pictures and play materials. The *SEN Toolkit* (p. 2) suggests that children should be enabled to understand the importance of information, express their feelings, take part in discussions and indicate their choices. They should be encouraged to set learning targets and contribute to IEPs, and to 'take part in all decision making processes that occur in education'. Superficial involvement is not sufficient. By learning to make simple choices and being consulted on daily matters from an early age children will gain greater confidence in their own opinions. This can be built into the daily routine for all young children in early years settings and staff should consider ways in which children can be naturally involved in planning and reviewing their own experiences.

Conclusion

Empowerment, entitlement, partnership, parental choice and access are recurrent themes in *Excellence for All Children* (DfEE 1997a) and the SEN *Programme of Action* (DfEE 1998). Placing parents first is essential to the future development of services aimed at supporting the young child. The power of parents to participate as equal partners in the cyclical process of assessment, provision and review stems from the relationship they share with the child. It is a relationship at the heart of early development which crosses artificial divides between care and education (Wolfendale 1997: 24). The processes of partnership are as important as the outcomes, and partnership with parents will continue to be challenging by its very nature. The organization as well as the individuals within it needs to develop a culture of partnership. Early years workers need to look for ways to use partnership proactively, as this will prevent confrontation developing. Parents need time and space to develop their own skills and experience as parents. Parents are people who know their children well.

We need to accept parents' expertise even if it appears at times to question our own. Parents also have a part to play and a responsibility to communicate regularly with the child's setting and alert staff to any concerns they have about their child's learning and development.

However, some commentators suggest that 'the whole coercive framework of special education continues to make nonsense of a rhetoric of parental involvement, partnership or choice' (Galloway *et al.* 1994: 129). Weatherley (1979), for example, identified three main difficulties with parents as participants in decision making. First, professionals usually outnumber them; second, they are outsiders in an ongoing group; and third, there may be a status difference in education and social class between parents and professionals. Consequently, it has been suggested that 'minimum practical recognition has been given to the validity and usefulness of their expertise and experiences' (Dale 1996: 5). Madden (1995) comments that, in spite of progress, many professionals continue to suffer from 'parentitis' – a mixture of prejudice, ambivalence and ignorance of the strengths, concerns and insights of parents. Parents of all children, not only those with SEN, need to play an active and valued role in their children's education and be given a real say in the way their child is educated. All that most parents want is for their children to have 'normal' childhood experiences. Appropriately, the last word in this chapter goes to a parent:

> My ideal world at the moment would be to have, erm, to educate people more to not be so ignorant of things and for Tom to be just ... I'd love him to be, I'll be crying in a minute [nervous laughter] I mean, erm, I – to tell them to be – I mean I love him to bits, but I'd love him to be normal but ... [silent pause as she sheds a few tears] although it's years I still find it hard – [sobbing].

7

Beyond the paintpots: inclusion and learning support assistants

Learning supporters are the blood transfusion of the education service.

(Hancock, cited in Rusteimer and Shaw 2001)

The Warnock Report (DES 1978) provided a catalyst for an increasing number of support staff to be employed in mainstream schools to support the education and care of children with SEN. These staff may be employed by the school in the broader role of a classroom assistant or funded by the LEA as a part of a child's special educational provision in the statement. Moyles (1997) describes them as 'Jills of all trades'; children often call them 'helpers'. They have a myriad of official job titles, including special needs assistants, learning support assistants (LSAs), classroom assistants, educational assistants and teaching assistants. They come from a variety of backgrounds with a range of qualifications. However, their common ground is that to a greater or lesser extent they are involved in supporting children's learning. Therefore the generic term used throughout this chapter is that of LSA. This chapter examines the role of the LSA in the context of supporting young children with SEN or disabilities.

It begins with a broad overview of the roles and responsibilities of LSAs, the majority of whom are employed in Key Stage 1 in primary schools. However, the emphasis on early identification and assessment and the continued drive for inclusive practices in early education settings in receipt of government funding is already prompting a similar specific role supporting individual children from increasingly younger ages. This is illustrated in the second part of the chapter which presents and reviews an innovative scheme in Warwickshire for supporting inclusion in early years settings in receipt of government funding, including pre-school voluntary groups and private nurseries as well as LEA maintained nursery schools or classes.

Initiatives to promote inclusion have resulted in a changing pattern of educational provision, and the number of adults working in mainstream classrooms alongside teachers increased by 48 per cent between 1995 and 2000. Within all stages of the graduated model of assessment and pro-vision there is a growing tendency to draw on extra adults to support children's learning. According to the *Times Educational Supplement* (18 October 2002) there were 213,000 support workers in schools and an extra 50,000 have been promised to be in place by 2006. Under govern-ment plans the number of support workers in schools will eventually equal the number of teachers. The growing interest in the role of LSAs has stemmed from this dramatic increase in their numbers combined with a growing recognition of the potentially crucial role an effectively managed LSA can play in promoting inclusion.

Traditionally associated with tasks such as washing paintpots, making costumes, sharpening pencils and mounting displays, the role of the extra adult in the early years classroom has gradually evolved to focus on supporting children's learning. The Green Paper (DfEE 1997a) described LSAs' tasks as helping children with reading difficulties, supporting speech therapy programmes and helping children with SEN access the curriculum. The SEN programme of action (DfEE 1998) asserts that the LSA can play a 'key role' in supporting pupils with a wide range of needs. Aird (2000) states that there can be little doubt that the LSA's role within the classroom is an important one but it is not always the case that the potential benefits of deploying LSAs are fully realized in practice. Several writers (Balshaw 1999; Farrell *et al.* 1999; Jones 2000; Papatheo-dorou *et al.* 2001) suggest that the nature and purpose of the role lacks clarity and consistency.

Balshaw (1999) provides a succinct analysis of the role and divides LSA tasks into two areas: child contact and non-contact. Child contact is subdivided into a further three areas: curriculum and learning related (including running small literacy or numeracy groups, helping children achieve IEP targets or supporting them with ICT); pastoral care (including listening to children and just being there for them); and physical support (e.g. administering first aid etc.). One study (Papa-theodorou *et al.* 2001) found, for example, that where LSAs are employed to support one particular child they can become rather protective, offering comfort, attention and reassurance, but had few constructive strategies for dealing with learning or behavioural difficulties. The quality of support appeared to depend on two factors: first, the willingness or otherwise of the class teacher or setting manager to view the LSA as a valued member of staff; and second, the nature of support received by children, which often depended on the personality, training, experience, qualifications and attitudes of the individual LSA (Papatheodorou *et al.* 2001). The non-contact aspects of the role include ancillary or preparation tasks including producing materials, recording television programmes, putting up displays and liaison or coordination tasks such as writing IEPs or attending reviews.

Principles for effective practice

Balshaw (1999) offers six interlocking principles for developing policy and practice. The first is linked to roles and responsibilities. She suggests that LSAs should be clear about their roles and responsibilities. The lack of clarity in the role of the LSA is a recurring theme in the debate. This may be because the role will vary according to the educational setting and the needs of the individual child or group of children. Nevertheless, the National Association for Special Educational Needs (NASEN 2001) points out that LSAs can 'reasonably expect that their role in each situation is clearly defined'. Balshaw further suggests that LSAs should be involved in drawing up their roles and responsibilities, and reviewing teaching staff, SENCOs and others working with LSAs should also be informed as to the expectations of the LSA role (1999: 13).

A second principle relates to communication. A report from Ofsted (1996) concluded that the most influential factor in the effectiveness of in-class support was the quality of joint planning between the class teacher and the LSA. Balshaw (1999: 12) suggests that 'learning support assistants should be included in and understand the communication system in the school' or setting and not be 'left in no man's land'. In practice this aspect of the role appears to be inconsistent. One LSA (Jones 2000) for example, describes how she was given no direct responsibility and was not asked to contribute to IEPs or reviews. She emphasized that she felt isolated, undervalued and uninformed: 'They never tell me anything. I never go to any meetings. I've never even seen the statement or anything ... I never get included in anything. Everyone had a daffodil [in the Mother's Day assembly]. What did I get? Nothing'.

On the other hand, another LSA observed by Jones (2000) had quite a different experience. The SENCO and the outside agencies had direct contact with the LSA rather than the class teacher. Similarly, parents also bypassed the class teacher and made direct contact with the LSA. It was the LSA who kept all the files and records of the children's IEPs. She had almost taken over complete responsibility for the children from the class teacher. In both cases a more balanced approach would have been more effective.

A third principle advanced by Balshaw (1999) is concerned with consistency of approach, including positive attitudes towards LSAs, viewing them as part of the provision to meet children's educational needs, not as general ancillary workers. It is also important that they do not see themselves merely as there to contain pupils' behaviour. The following quotes from LSAs (Jones 2000) suggest this may sometimes be the case:

> Well, he just gets my support to keep him out of mischief really. He doesn't need anything special really.

> Well, I wouldn't say he needs me sitting by him all the time, but I feel that he still looks for me. And if he knows I'm there he's okay. If I wasn't there, then he'd start messing about.

Both NASEN (2001) and Balshaw (1999) suggest team membership is crucial to the success of the LSA role. The experience and knowledge of LSAs should be recognized and their contributions valued by other team members. LSAs need a sense of belonging to a professional team rather than the sense of isolation felt in the following quote from an LSA whose job title was 'integration assistant':

> An integration assistant position can be a very lonely and isolated one. As one is only allocated so many hours each day you never feel part of the school. You are neither a teacher nor a classroom ancillary, so you sometimes feel in the twilight zone between the two.

Balshaw (1999: 10) offers a possible explanation as to why LSAs feel segregated, suggesting a link with the language of SEN, and asserting that where children are described as having difficulties and disabilities, or are singled out and labelled by teaching staff and others such as parents, governors and other children and students, then clearly the assistants working specifically with them are part of that segregated and individualizing culture.

Finally, Balshaw (1999) suggests that LSAs should be encouraged to develop personal and professional skills and also that their staff development needs should be supported. NASEN (2001) strengthens this into giving LSAs a right to professional development and support. They should be enabled to develop the sound knowledge and skills base needed for the role. NASEN suggests that such training should include SEN awareness, core and specialist skills and that LSAs have the right to receive information, induction and support within the workplace. A good starting point would be for settings and schools to consult the LSAs themselves and work with them in developing policy and practice in the implementation of learning support throughout the school.

Inclusion and learning support

Undoubtedly, the provision of LSAs has enabled many more children with statements of SEN to attend mainstreams schools. A headteacher's comment illustrates this point: 'It is vital that Alan receives immediate support in terms of ancillary help in the classroom if he is to survive in mainstream education. His problems are worsened by lack of resources and the one-to-one situation he desperately requires'.

However, the mere presence of an LSA does not guarantee inclusion and can actually lead to exclusive practices. Concern is greater where the LSA is allocated to support a specific child for a substantial number of hours each week. It could be, for example, that the LSA becomes a substitute for the teacher. The LSA may be seen as assuming responsibility for the child to the point that the teacher feels resentful if the LSA is not there. This can reinforce the idea that the presence of children with SEN is a problem. In the following quote the LSA did not view the children as part of the class but rather as an added 'extra': 'But when I'm not there the teacher has the hassle of looking after two extra children'. The reception teacher agreed: 'She was shared at first but they needed one each. If she was morning with one and afternoon with the other, what did you do the rest of the day with them?'

Several concerns have been raised that LSAs may act as a barrier between young people with special needs and other pupils. The danger is that LSA provision can lead to pupils with significant needs becoming marginalized from ordinary experiences. Studies have found that, unless effectively managed, the presence of the LSA can actually inhibit rather than facilitate interaction between the child and children without special needs. Children who worked mostly with LSAs on a one-to-one basis had limited opportunities for collaboration and interactions with their peers (Papatheodorou *et al.* 2001). The presence of the LSA also seemed to contribute towards the loss of the pupils' ability to work independently. If the LSA is part-time, how does the pupil learn and behave when the LSA is not there? One study which set out to compare a child's behaviour and learning experiences in the mornings, with the presence of an LSA, with his experiences in the afternoons in her absence found there was a stark contrast between the child's social, behavioural and academic performance in the mornings as compared to the afternoons, with the child segregated for almost 50 per cent of his time in school (Papatheodorou *et al.* 2001). However, the headteacher thought this same case was a shining example of inclusion, saying that: 'Alan now has help each morning and this has been very beneficial to him'. In spite of these setbacks there are many examples of LSAs being the keystone of inclusive practice. The next section reviews a model for using LSAs to support inclusion in preschool settings in Warwickshire.

Supporting inclusion through a flexible budget

This section is based on a small-scale study of a Warwickshire-based initiative aimed at supporting inclusion in the early years through a flexible budget system. The flexible budget system is based on a framework whereby certain children with SEN are supported in mainstream early education settings by an additional adult, over and above the normal staffing ratios. Money is allocated from the flexible budget for a number of hours each week to pay for individual support for a particular child (or more than one child, if appropriate) within an early education setting, during the child's preschool year. Early education settings include nursery classes and nursery schools in the maintained sector and other providers – for example, private day nurseries and preschools and playgroups in receipt of government grant funding for nursery places. The study, conducted in 2002, gathered information through interviews with preschool SEN teachers, questionnaires to settings, questionnaires to flexible budget assistants (FBAs) and a range of documentary evidence. The emerging themes are used to identify challenges and issues for further consideration in the broader policy and practice contexts.

The flexible budget system, designed to provide a source of funding for an LSA to give a child one-to-one support, is accessed through Warwickshire's Disability, Illness, Sensory and Communication Service (DISCS) preschool SEN teachers. The money from the flexible budget is used to pay the FBA for a certain number of hours a week. The FBA is employed directly by the setting. It is intended that the number of hours, where possible, should be managed down as the year progresses. In the period April 2001 to March 2002, the scheme enabled 74 children under 5 to receive additional support, 50 of whom had previous involvement with the child development centre. The use of the flexible budget means that almost all children's needs can be met at the preschool stage without requiring statutory assessment.

Training and qualifications

Two-thirds of FBAs in the scheme had some type of early years qualification or had attended some training. All settings said they would release their helper for training and all FBAs said they would attend specific training. The FBAs ranged from those who were very well qualified and experienced to those who were unqualified and for whom it was their first time working with a SEN child. In almost all instances the FBA was supported and trained 'on the job' within the setting. While recognizing the differing nature of each child's needs for support there were a number of common and generic issues which could best be addressed through group or cluster training. It would have been ideal if the training could be accredited in some way and linked with training for LSAs in Key Stage 1. This would set a minimum level of the quality and attach value and status to the role. The study found that the great majority of children were being supported due to behavioural or speech and language difficulties, and suggested these areas should be a priority in specific training. It suggested that group or geographical cluster training in contributing to writing IEPs and assessment would also have been useful and would enable FBAs to network with each other, sharing knowledge, experiences and resources.

The role of the FBA

Although there were some contextual variations the role of the FBA was similar in most settings. The main areas of responsibility included supporting children in one-to-one or small groups in the daily routine; supporting children in moving towards IEP targets; encouraging and modelling appropriate behaviour; and helping children access the foundation stage curriculum. Other tasks included playing with and sharing books with children to develop language skills, preparing resources and maintaining child safety. However, only 20 per cent of settings had a written role description for the FBA. In other words, 80 per cent of those employed had no written role description. The most commonly cited ways in which the FBAs thought their role could be made more effective were by undertaking specific and general training – for example, on observation techniques – by working more hours and by being able to collect more structured observations.

Two thirds of settings taking part in the scheme did not have any formal system of monitoring the FBA. Appreciating the differences between different children's needs, a generic role description would have been useful. This could provide a model for settings to adapt to their own contexts. The study recommended that some sort of annual self-evaluation scheme would also provide information on the successful or less successful aspects of the flexible budget scheme.

The study found that one third of setting managers or nursery headteachers thought that the flexible budget system had enabled the setting to include a child who may otherwise have been excluded. All settings stated that the flexible budget had enabled them to support the child more effectively than might otherwise have been possible and all said they would a participate again in the future. There were clearly hidden benefits of the scheme in terms of attitudes to inclusion.

Recruitment and retention

The questionnaires showed clearly that over 95 per cent of settings employed an FBA who was already known to them. Two thirds of the FBAs had worked in the setting before, either employed or on a voluntary basis. Just under half were parents of children attending the setting. The majority worked for five to ten hours per week. Almost all FBAs found the position through word of mouth with only one responding to an advert. The main reasons given for taking the post were because it enhanced professional development, fitted in with family commitments or because they were interested in working with children. Almost all (over 95 per cent) had worked with children before in some context but for two thirds it was their first experience of working with a child with SEN. The scheme has therefore created a newly experienced and developing workforce – but the small number who would definitely be carrying on was a cause for concern. Over half of the settings did not know if their FBA would be with them the following September. Only 25 per cent of FBAs said they would be remaining in the setting. Therefore three quarters of the assistants may simply 'evaporate' – the same proportion that said they would like to carry on if work were available. The review suggested that a system should be developed to record their details for future employment or redeployment, and consideration should be given to employing or retaining a small 'core' group of support workers – for example, one per geographical area. These FBAs could be trained to help the SEN teacher, prepare resources and so on, if no direct hours were available. If effort is put into training these people it will be wasted if they are not retained in the service.

The team of SEN preschool teachers or area SENCOs played a positive role in enabling the success of the scheme. The key ways identified were in giving general advice and suggesting strategies or resources for helping the child; contributing to IEP planning and reviews; observing children, and providing helpful literature.

The benefits to the children could not be measured systematically. Although progress was reviewed through IEPs it is unclear how much can be attributed to the presence of the FBA. There was no formal system in place for measuring the benefits in terms of pupil progress as compared to progress that would have been made without support. However, responses suggested that the following benefits had occurred (the frequency with which these were mentioned indicates high reliability): children showed more acceptable social skills and improved ability to cope with new situations; an increased ability to play and talk with other children; improved listening, attention and concentration skills; improved ability to participate in activities; more confidence and independence; improved behaviour; less frustration and more willingness to take turns or accept rules and routines. Almost all the children participating in the scheme showed improved language and communication skills.

Overall, the flexible budget system worked well, not least due to the hard work, flexibility, knowledge and experience of the SEN teachers under strong leadership. However, there were some areas emerging from the evidence which need further consideration to improve things still further, such as resolving the recruitment and retention issue. As is the case with LSAs in schools, more explicit guidance for the role of the SENCO teacher and the FBA would be beneficial. Again, as with LSAs, structured training and professional development for FBAs should be a priority in areas of highest referral, and this could be made a condition of receiving the budget. The evaluation recommended that in schemes of this type a simple service level agreement-type document could be drawn up explaining what is expected from the setting in return for the budget and what the setting can expect from the local support service. In all such initiatives it would be important to consider arrangements on transition to school – for example, whether support should be continued until statutory school age, or in cases where a continued high level of support is required, until statutory assessment is completed.

Conclusion

There appears to be an unresolved dilemma regarding the traditional 'ancillary' role of a classroom helper in supporting teachers' work, usually associated with mundane tasks such as sharpening pencils and mounting displays, versus the recently developed role associated with supporting children's learning. This is exacerbated by the lack of a systematic local and national framework for professional and career development, a national pay structure and any explicit definition of LSA roles and responsibilities. There is a need for a single profession of assistants with a unified career structure (Farrell *et al.* 1999).

There is also a need for training, preferably accredited, of support workers to gain a clear understanding of what inclusion and inclusive learning are meant to be, and how their role should be interpreted and implemented within such an understanding. The subtle segregation of children with special needs supported on a one-to-one basis may only highlight the differences among individuals and contribute to prejudice formation among youngsters. Inclusion is not about locational integration, it is about participation in all aspects of the educational setting's work, relationships and life.

Moreover, if children with statements are spending substantial amounts of the school day with their assistants, the quality of the contact needs to be monitored and supported in order to develop inclusive practice. The inhibition of the naturally occurring interactions and relationships between children with special needs and their classmates might be prove to be a damaging practice. Those working with LSAs need training in skills and competencies in order to achieve inclusive practices that will allow young children with special needs to actively participate in all aspects of work according to their abilities and strengths.

LSAs can play a pivotal role in the process of inclusion. New initiatives to include young children in mainstream early education settings with support but without the need for a statutory assessment, are to be welcomed and the Warwickshire scheme shows how, if given the resources, training and support, many more children under 5 could access effective inclusive learning environments. Finally, in the words of a speaker at a conference for learning supporters:

It is ironic that a group of people who themselves feel excluded and unrecognised – the learning supporters – are the ones trying to help disabled and other previously excluded young people to be included in mainstream education and society. It's really difficult to understand how this situation has happened without recognising the struggle that the world is having with the concept of inclusion.

(Micheline Mason, cited in Rusteimer and Shaw 2001)

Conclusion

> It is of the utmost importance that a backward child should receive appropriate help at the earliest possible moment.
>
> (DES 1964: 5)

This book, based largely on the perspectives of early years practitioners involved in identifying and assessing young children with SEN, has suggested that professional responses to the *Code of Practice* (DfES 2001a) are based on a general conviction that early identification is a positive move. It has demonstrated how early identification is perceived to protect the interests of vulnerable children, ensuring that their needs are recognized. However, it has argued that there is a need to move away from values, language and practices that maintain a focus on individual deficit, to policy and practice that considers young children's learning within a broader context. It has suggested that the principle of inclusion, dominant at the level of political rhetoric, is being undermined by a continued use of policies, procedures and terms that perpetuate responses based on the idea that some children are 'normal' and others 'special'. This encourages a narrow focus on small groups of children, rather than a reappraisal of early childhood education as part of an effort to improve education for all children.

The principles of the *Code* (DfES 2001a) are welcome in that they assert the importance of assessing needs early, of entitlement to the foundation stage curriculum and inclusive education. However, unless our responses focus on these principles and the processes of supporting children, rather than the mechanics of the procedures, any consideration of broader issues may be overlooked. The early years SENCO role, with its formidable list of responsibilities, is pivotal in developing revised policies based on articulated beliefs, values and principles to ensure that the educational outcomes of assessment are positive and inclusive, rather than separate and marginalizing. It is the collective responsibility of all early years practitioners to support and empower children with SEN and their parents. This book has been based on the conviction that 'The principles which inform early years education can be seen to provide for the whole of education a model of genuine inclusion' (Lloyd 1997: 172). Therefore, it is up to those working with young children to continue to lead the way in challenging the attitudes and assumptions underlying policy and practice – attitudes which may ultimately determine children's experiences not only in the early years but for the rest of their lives.

Useful addresses

Advisory Centre for Education (ACE)
Unit 1B, Aberdeen Studios
22 Highbury Grove
London N5 2DQ
Tel: 0207 354 8321
Freephone helpline: 0808 800 5793, 2–5 p.m. weekdays
Website: www.ace-ed.org.uk
A national advice centre for parents offering information and support about state education in England and Wales for 5- to 16-year-olds.

Afasic
2nd Floor, 50–52 Great Sutton St
London EC1V 0DJ
Helpline: 0845 355 5577
The UK charity representing children and young adults with communication impairments.

Association of Speech and Language Therapists (ASLTIP)
Coleheath Bottom
Speen
Princes Risborough
Bucks HP27 0S2
Tel: 0870 241 3357

British Dyslexia Association
98 London Road
Reading RG1 5AU
Tel: 0118 966 2677
Helpline: 0118 966 8271
Website: www.bda-dyslexia.org.uk

British Stammering Association
15 Old Ford Road
London E2 9PJ
Tel: 0208 983 1003

Centre for Accessible Environments
Nutmeg House
60 Gainsford Street
London SE1 2NY
Tel: 0207 357 8182

Centre for Studies on Inclusive Education
Room 2S203 S Block
Frenchay Campus
Coldharbour Lane
Bristol BS16 1QU
Tel: 0117 344 4007

Contact a Family (CAF)
209–211 City Road
London ECIV IJN
Tel: 020 7608 8700
Freephone helpline: 0808 808 3555
Provides support and advice to parents of children with special needs.

Council for Disabled Children
8 Wakley Street
London EC1V 7QE
Tel: 020 7843 6061
Email: cdc@ncb.org.uk
Website: www.nch.org.uk/cdc.htm

Department for Education and Skills (DfES) Early Years & Childcare Unit
DfES
Caxton House
6–12 Tothill Street
London SW1H 9NA
Tel: 020 72735754
Fax: 020 7273 5745
E-mail: early.years@dfes.gov.uk

DfES Early Years Census queries
DfES
Mowden Hall
Staindrop Road
Darlington DL3 9BG
Tel: 01325 392626
Fax: 01325 392211

DfES Early Education (*formerly known as British Association for Early Childhood Education (BAECE)*)
136 Cavell Street
London E1 2JA
Tel: 020 7539 5400
Fax: 020 7539 5409
E-mail: office@early-education.org.uk
Website: www.early-education.org.uk

DfES Publications Centre
PO Box 5050
Sudbury
Suffolk CO10 6ZQ
Tel: 0845 602 2260
Fax: 0845 603 3360
E-mail: dfes@prolog.uk.com

DIAL-UK (Disablement Information and Advice Lines)
St Catherines
Tickhill Road
Doncaster DN4 8QN
Tel: 01302 310123 to find out who your local officer is.
Supports a network of local disablement information and advice officers.

Disabled Living Foundation
380–384 Harrow Road
London W9 2HU
Tel: 0207 289 6111
Helpline: 0845 130 9177

Down's Syndrome Association
155 Mithcam Road
Tooting
London SW17 9PG
Tel: 0208 682 4001
Website: www.downs-syndrome.org.uk

Dyscovery Centre
New Surgery
4 Church Road
Whitchurch
Cardiff CF14 2DZ
Tel: 029 2062 8222
The centre assesses and treats children with dyspraxia but can also help
with information.

Dyspraxia Foundation
8 West Alley
Hitchin
Herts SG5 1EG
Tel. 01462 454986
Website: www.emmbrook.demon.co.uk/dysprax/homepage.htm

Home-Start UK
2 Salisbury Road
Leicester LE1 7QR
Tel: 0116 233 9955
Website: www.home-start.org.uk

Kidsactive *(formerly HAPA)*
Pryor's Bank
Bishop's Park
London SW6 3LA
Tel: 0207 731 1435 & 020 7736 4443
National charity providing information and training on inclusive play.

LOOK *(part of the National Federation of Families with Visually Impaired Children)*
Queen Alexander College
49 Court Oak Road
Harborne
Birmingham B17 9TG
Tel: 0121 428 5038
Website: www.look-uk.org

MENCAP
123 Golden Lane
London EC17 ORT
Tel: 0207 454 0454
Can advise on working with children with learning difficulties.

National Association for Special Educational Needs (NASEN)
NASEN House
4/5 Amber Business Village
Amber Close
Amington
Tamworth B77 4RP
Tel: 01827 311500
Website: www.nasen.org.uk

National Autistic Society
393 City Road
London EC1V 1NE
Tel: 0207 903 3599
Helpline: 0207 903 3555

National Deaf Children's Society
15 Dufferin Street
London EC1Y 8PD
Tel/minicom: 0808 800 8880
Can advise on communicating with deaf children.

National Portage Association
PO Box 3075
Yeovil
Somerset BA21 3JE
Tel: 01935 471641
Website: www.portage.org.uk

Parents for Inclusion
Unit 2
70 South Lambeth Road
London SW8 1RL
Tel: 0207 735 7735
An organization set up by parents of disabled children to provide support and advice to parents and to campaign for the inclusion of disabled children in mainstream education.

Partially Sighted Society
Queen's Road
Doncaster DN1 2NX
Tel: 01302 323132

Qualifications and Curriculum Authority (QCA)
83 Piccadilly
London W1J 8QA
Tel: 020 7509 5555

Royal College of Speech and Language Therapists
2–3 White Hart Yard
London SE1 1NX
Tel: 020 7378 1200

Royal National Institute for the Blind (RNIB)
105 Judd Street
London WC1H 9NE
Tel: 0207 388 1266
Can advise on many aspects of play and leisure for visually impaired children.

Scope
6 Market Road
London N7 9PW
Helpline: 0808 800 3333
Provides support for children with cerebral palsy and related disabilities, their parents and carers.

References

Abberley, P. (1992) The concept of oppression and the development of a social theory of disability, in T. Booth, V. Swann, M. Masterton and P. Potts (eds) *Learning For All, 2 – Policies for Diversity in Education.* London: Routledge.

Ainscow, M. (1988) Beyond the eyes of the monster: an analysis of recent trends in assessment and recording, *Support for Learning*, 3(3): 149–59.

Ainscow, M. (1991) Effective schools for all: an alternative approach to special needs in education, in M. Ainscow (ed.) *Effective Schools For All.* London: David Fulton.

Aird, R. (2000) The case of specialist training for learning support assistants employed in schools for children with severe, profound and multiple learning difficulties, *Support for Learning*, 15(3): 106–10.

Appleton, P.L. and Minchom, P.E. (1991) Models of parent partnership and child development centres, *Child: Care, Health and Development*, (17): 27–38.

Armstrong, D. (1996) *The Management of Special and Inclusive Education: An Historical Overview: Unit Three.* Sheffield: University of Sheffield.

Ballard, K. (ed.) (1999) *Inclusive Education: International Voices on Disability and Justice.* London: Falmer Press.

Balshaw, M. (1999) *Help in the Classroom*, 2nd edn. London: David Fulton.

Barton, L. (1999) Market ideologies, education and the challenge for inclusion, in H. Daniels and P. Garner (eds) *Inclusive Education.* London: Kogan Page.

Barton, L. and Oliver, M. (1992) Special needs: personal trouble or public issue? in M. Arnott and L. Barton (eds) *Voicing Concerns.* Wallingford: Triangle Books.

Barton, L. and Tomlinson, S. (eds) (1981) *Special Education: Policy, Practices and Social Issues.* London: Harper & Row.

Booth, T. and Ainscow, M. (2002) *Index for Inclusion.* Bristol: CSIE.

Booth, T., Ainscow, M. and Dyson, A. (1997) Understanding inclusion and exclusion in the English competitive education system, *International Journal of Inclusive Education*, 1(4): 337–55.

Buckley, S. (1994) Early intervention: the state of the art, in B. Carpenter (ed.) *Early Intervention: Where Are We Now?* Oxford: Westminster Press.

Carpenter, B. (1996) Enabling partnership: families and schools, in B. Carpenter, R. Ashdown and K. Bovair (eds) *Enabling Access: Effective Teaching and Learning for Pupils with Learning Difficulties*. London: David Fulton.

Chasty, H. and Friel, J. (1991) *Children with Special Needs – Assessment, Law and Practice: Caught in the Act*. London: Jessica Kingsley.

Children Act (1989) London: HMSO.

Clark, C., Dyson, A. and Millward, A. (1990) Evolution or revolution: dilemmas in the post ERA management of special educational needs by local authorities, *Oxford Review of Education*, 16(3): 279–89.

Conner, C. (1991) *Assessment and Testing in the Primary School*. Basingstoke: Falmer Press.

Crowther, D., Dyson, A., Lin, M. and Millward, A. (1997) *The Role of the Special Educational Needs Co-ordinator in Schools: Analytical Report*. Newcastle upon Tyne: University of Newcastle.

CSIE (Centre for Studies on Inclusive Education) (1999) *Developing an Inclusive Policy for Your School: A CSIE guide*. Bristol: CSIE.

Cunningham, C. and Davis, H. (1985) *Working with Parents: Frameworks for Collaboration*. Buckingham: Open University Press.

Dale, N. (1996) *Working with Families of Children with Special Educational Needs: Partnership and Practice*. London: Routledge.

Davis, H. (1985) Developing the role of parent adviser in the child health service, in E. D'Ath and G. Pugh (eds) *Partnership Paper 3*. London: National Children's Bureau.

DES (Department of Education and Science) (1964) Education Pamphlet No.46: *Slow Learners at School*. London: HMSO.

DES (Department of Education and Science) (1978) *Special Educational Needs: Report of the Committee of Enquiry into the Education of Handicapped Children and Young People* (the Warnock Report). London: HMSO.

DfE (Department for Education) (1994) *The Code of Practice on the Identification and Assessment of Special Educational Needs*. London: DfE.

DfEE (Department for Education and Employment) (1997a) *Excellence for All Children: Meeting Special Educational Needs*. London: The Stationery Office.

DfEE (Department for Education and Employment) (1997b) *The SENCO Guide*. London: The Stationery Office.

DfEE (Department for Education and Employment) (1998) *Meeting Special Educational Needs: A Programme of Action*. London: DfEE.

DfEE/QCA (Department for Education and Employment/Qualifications and Curriculum Authority) (2000) *Curriculum Guidance for the Foundation Stage*. Suffolk: QCA.

DfES (Department for Education and Skills) (2001a) *Special Educational Needs Code of Practice*. Nottingham: DfES.

DfES (Department for Education and Skills) (2001b) *National Standards for Under Eights Daycare and Childminding*. Nottingham: DfES.

DfES (Department for Education and Skills) (2001c) *SEN Toolkit*. Nottingham: DfES.

DfES (Department for Education and Skills) (2001d) *Special Educational Needs (SEN): A Guide for Parents and Carers*. Nottingham: DfES.

DfES (Department for Education and Skills) (2002) *Requirements of Nursery Education Grant 2002–2003*. Nottingham: DfES.

DfES (Department for Education and Skills) (2003) *Foundation Stage Profile*. Suffolk: QCA.

Disability Discrimination Act (DDA) (1995) London: The Stationery Office.

Edgington, M. (1998) *The Nursery Teacher in Action*. London: Paul Chapman Publishing.

Education Act (1981) London: HMSO.

Education Act (1996) London: The Stationery Office.

Education Act (1997) London: The Stationery Office.

Farrell, P., Balshaw, M. and Polat, F. (1999) *The Management, Role and Training of Learning Support Assistants*. London: DfEE.

Forest, M. and Pearpoint, J. (1992) Two roads: inclusion or exclusion, in J. Pearpoint, M. Forest and J. Snow (eds) *The Inclusion Papers: Strategies to Make Inclusion Work*. Toronto: Inclusion Press.

Fulcher, G. (1989) *Disabling Policies? A Comparative Approach to Education Policy and Disability*. Lewes: Falmer Press.

Fulcher, G. (1990) Students with special needs: lessons from comparisons, *Journal of Education Policy*, 5(4): 347–58.

Galloway, D., Armstrong, D. and Tomlinson, S. (1994) *The Assessment of Special Educational Needs, Whose Problem?* London: Longman.

Gascoigne, E. (1995) *Working with Parents as Partners in SEN*. London: David Fulton.

Gipps, C. and Stobart, G. (1993) *Assessment: A Teachers' Guide to the Issues*. London: Hodder & Stoughton.

Goacher, B., Evans, J., Welton, J. and Wedell, K. (1988) *Policy and Provision for Special Educational Needs: Implementing the 1981 Education Act*. London: Cassell.

Hegarty, S. (1993) *Special Needs in Ordinary Schools*. London: Cassell.

Heward, C. and Lloyd-Smith, M. (1990) Assessing the impact of legislation on special education policy – an historical analysis, *Journal of Education Policy*, 5(1): 21–36.

Jones, C. (1998) Early intervention: the eternal triangle? in K. Stalker and C. Robinson (eds) *Growing up with Disability*. London: Jessica Kingsley.

Jones, C. (2000) Special educational needs: identification and assessment in the early years. PhD thesis, University of Warwick, April.

Lewis, A. (1995) *Children's Understanding of Disability*. London: Routledge.

Lewis, A. (1996) Summative National Curriculum assessments of primary aged children with special needs, *British Journal of Special Education*, 23(1): 9–14.

Lewis, A., Neill, S.R. St. J. and Campbell, R.J. (1996) *The Implementation of the Code of Practice in Primary and Secondary Schools: A National Survey of Perceptions of Special Educational Needs Co-ordinators*. Coventry: Institute of Education, University of Warwick.

Lindsay, G. (1998) Baseline assessment: a positive or malign initiative? in B. Norwich and G. Lindsay (eds) *Baseline Assessment*. Tamworth: NASEN.

Lindsay, G. (2000) Baseline assessment: how can it help? in H. Daniels (ed.) *Special Education Re-formed*. London: Falmer Press.

Lindsay, G. and Desforges, M. (1998) *Baseline Assessment: Practice, Problems and Possibilities*. London: David Fulton.

Lloyd, C. (1997) Inclusive education for children with special educational needs in the early years, in S. Wolfendale (ed.) *Meeting Special Needs in the Early Years*. London: David Fulton.

Luton, K. (1995) *Policy Development for Special Educational Needs: A Primary School Approach*. Tamworth: NASEN.

Madden, P. (1995) Parents as partners: a new perspective, *British Journal of Learning Disabilities*, 23: 27.

Mason, M. (1992) The integration alliance: background and manifesto, in T. Booth, V. Swann, M. Masterton and P. Potts (eds) *Policies for Diversity in Education*. London: Routledge.

Mittler, P. and Mittler, H. (eds) (1994) *Innovations in Family Support for People with Learning Disabilities*. Lancashire: Lisieux Hall.

Moss, G. (ed.) (1996) *Effective Management of Special Needs*. Birmingham: The Questions Publishing Company Ltd.

Moyles, J. (with Suschitzky, W.) (1997) 'Jills of all Trades': Classroom Assistants in KS1 Classes. London: Association of Teachers and Lecturers.

NASEN (National Association for Special Educational Needs) (2001) *Policy Document on Learning Support Assistants*. Tamworth: NASEN.

Ofsted (Office for Standards in Education) (1996) *The Implementation of the Code of Practice for Pupils with Special Educational Needs*. London: HMSO.

Oliver, M. (1990) Politics and language: the need for a new understanding. *International Rehabilitation Review*, XL (April): 10.

Panter, S. (1995) *How to Survive as an SEN Co-ordinator*. Lichfield: Qed.

Papatheodorou, T., Jones, C. and Boggis, A. (2001) Learning support, assistants in early years settings: the challenge for inclusive education, *International Journal of Early Childhood*, Update 108, Spring.

Pickup, M. (1995) Role of the special educational needs co-ordinator: developing philosophy and practice, *Support for Learning*, 10(2): 88–92.

Plowden Report (1967) *Children and their Primary Schools*. London: HMSO.

Pound, L. (1999) *Supporting Mathematical Development in the Early Years*. Buckingham: Open University Press.

Roffey, S. (1999) *Special Needs in the Early Years: Collaboration, Communication and Coordination*. London: David Fulton.

Rusteimer, S. (with Shaw, L.) (2001) *Learning Supporters and Inclusion: Next Steps Forward*. Bristol: CSIE.

Satterly, D. (1989) *Assessment in Schools*. Oxford: Blackwell.

SCAA (School Curriculum and Assessment Authority) (1996) *Nursery Education: Desirable Outcomes for Children's Learning on Entering Compulsory Education*. London: SCAA/DfEE.

Shearer, M.S. and Shearer, D.E. (1972) The Portage project: a model for early childhood education, *Exceptional Children*, 36: 217.

Simmons, K. (1994) Decoding a new message, *British Journal of Special Education*, 21(2): 56–9.

Sinclair-Taylor, A. (1995) A 'dunce's' place: pupils' perceptions of the role of a special unit, *Educational Review*, 47(3): 263–74.

Slee, R. (ed.) (1993) *Is There a Desk with My Name on It? The Politics of Integration*. London: Falmer Press.

Soder, M. (1992) Disabilities as a social construct: the labelling approach revisited, in T. Booth, V. Swann, M. Masterton and P. Potts (eds) *Policies for Diversity in Education*. London: Routledge.

Sure Start (2003) *Birth to Three Matters: A Framework to Support Children in their Earliest Years*. Sure Start.

Taylor, T. (1977) *A New Partnership for Our Schools: Report of the Committee on School Management and Government*. London: HMSO.

TGAT (Task Group on Assessment and Testing) (1988) *A Report*. London: DES.

Tomlinson, S. (1982) *A Sociology of Special Education*. London: Routledge & Kegan Paul.

TTA (Teacher Training Agency) (1998) *National Standards for Special Educational Needs Co-ordinators*. London: TTA.

United Nations (1989) *UN Convention on the Rights of the Child*. London: UNICEF.

Vincent, C., Evans, J., Lunt, I. and Young P. (1996) Professionals under pressure: the administration of special education in a changing context, *British Educational Research Journal*, 22(4): 475–91.

Warnock, M. (1982) Children with special needs in ordinary schools: integration revisited, *Education Today*, 32(3): 56–61.

Warnock, M. (1985) Teacher, teach thyself (1985 Dimbleby Lecture), *The Listener*, 28 March: 10–14.

WCC (Warwickshire County Council) (2001) *Guidance for Early Education Settings in Warwickshire*. Warwick: Warwickshire Early Years Development and Childcare Partnership.

Weatherley, R. (1979) *Reforming Special Education: Policy Implementation from State Level to Street Level*. Cambridge, MA: Massachusetts Institute of Technology.

Welton, J., Wedell, K. and Vorhaus, G. (1982) *Meeting Special Needs: The 1981 Education Act and its Implications*. London: Institute of Education, University of London.

Withers, R. and Lee, J. (1988) Power in disguise, in L. Barton (ed.) *The Politics of Special Educational Needs*. Lewes: Falmer Press.

Wolfendale, S. (1983) *Parental Participation in Children's Development and Education*. London: Gordon & Breach Science Publishers.

Wolfendale, S. (1992) *Empowering Parents and Teachers: Working for Children*. London: Cassell.

Wolfendale, S. (1993) *Baseline Assessment – A Review of Current Practice: Issues and Strategies for Effective Implementation*. Stoke-on-Trent: Trentham Books.

Wolfendale, S. (ed.) (1989) *Parental Involvement: Developing Networks Between School, Home and Community*. London: Cassell.

Wolfendale, S. (ed.) (1997) *Working with Parents of Children with SEN after the Code of Practice*. London: David Fulton.

Index

Page numbers in *italics* refer to tables.

administrative role, SENCO 74–5
  burden of 76
  management of 79–82
Ainscow, M. 15, 28
  Booth, T. and 15, 16, 19–20
Appleton, P.L. and Minchom, P.E.
    89–90, 91
Armstrong, D. 14, 22
assessment
  baseline 26–7
  as decision-making process 34–5
  definitions 27, 28–9
  for *Early Years Action* 38–40
  formative 27–31
  graduated model 35–7
  as a lifelong process 25–6
  request, and written statement 47–8
  summative 31–2
attention deficit 39

Balshaw, M. 102, 103, 104–5
barriers to inclusion 15–16
Barton, L. 13, 15

and Oliver, M. 51
and Tomlinson, S. 9
baseline assessment 26–7
behavioural difficulties 39
Birth to Three Matters (Sure Start) 14
Booth, T.
  and Ainscow, M. 15, 16, 19–20
  et al. 14, 15

Carpenter, B. 92
case examples
  creating inclusive cultures 17–18
  partnerships 95, 96–8
  professional perceptions 48–50
Centre for Studies on Inclusive
    Education (CSIE) 20, 52, 59–60
Chasty, H. and Friel, J. 34
child contact role, LSA 102–3
Child Development Centre (CDC) 25
child involvement in decision-making
    98–9
child-child relationships 17–18, 105, 110
  see also inclusion

childminder networks 73
Children Act (1989) 9, 86–7, 98
child's rights 98
Clarke, C. *et al.* 53
Code of Practice (DfE/DfES) 1–2, 3–4,
    12, 15, 112–13
    assessment 21, 22, 23, 29, 30, 33,
        35–6, 48, 51
    child's wishes 99
    intervention 37, 39–40
    partnership 88–9, 92
    policy issues 52–3, 54, 55, 56–9, 62
    SENCO 72–4, 75–6, 78, 79, 83, 84–5
communication between staff
    liaison role, SENCO 75, 76, 83
    and LSA 103–4
compensatory view 22
complaints procedures 63
complexity of SEN 7–9
consent, parental 25, 40, 47, 93–4
consistency of approach, LSA 104
consumer model of partnership 91
continuous assessment 27–31
Crowther, D. *et al.* 55, 76, 77, 78
CSIE *see* Centre for Studies on
    Inclusive Education
Cunningham, C. and Davis, H. 89, 91
*Curriculum Guidance for the Foundation
    Stage* (DfEE/QCA) 1, 3

Dale, N. 88, 89–90, 91–2, 100
decision-making
    assessment as 34–5
    involvement of child 98–9
    involvement of parents 54
definitions
    assessment 27, 28–9
    learning difficulties 8
    parent 86–7
    partnership 88–9
    special educational provision 8–9
    see also language; models
Department for Education (DfE) *see*
    Code of Practice
Department for Education and

Employment (DfEE) 1, 3, 11–12,
    22, 23, 99, 102
Department of Education and Science
    (DES) 5, 112
    see also Warnock Report
Department for Education and Science
    (DfES) 93
    Foundation Stage Profile 3, 26, 27, 28
    see also Code of Practice
difference
    'identity of difference' 50
    responding to 13–14
Disability Discrimination Act (1995) 9
disability models
    inclusion *vs* segregation 9–11
    medical 9–10, 11, 16, 22

early identification 21–5
    information about 63–4
    see also labelling
Early Years Action 38–40, 41, 47
    IEP 41, 42–4
    triggers for implementation 37, 38
Early Years Action Plus 40
    IEP 41, 42, 44
    parental consent 40, 47, 93–4
    SENCO role 40, 83
    and statutory assessment 47
    triggers for implementation 40, 44
Edgington, M. 62, 63
Education Act(s) 2, 3, 25–6, 93
    (1981) 5, 8, 11, 34, 87
Education Reform Act (1988) 2, 31
effective practice
    LSA 103–5
    SENCO 83
emotional difficulties 39
    IEP 46
empowerment model of partnership 91
'evaluative' assessment 31–2
Excellence for All Children (DfEE) 3, 99
expert model of partnership 90
expert role, SENCO 75
external agencies 19, 37, 64–5
    see also Early Years Action Plus

finance
  barriers to inclusion 16
  flexible budget system 106–9
flexible budget assistant (FBA) 106
  recruitment and retention 108–9
  role 107–8
  training and qualifications 107
formative assessment 27–31
Foundation Stage Profile (DfES) 3, 26, 27, 28
Fulcher, G. 10, 15, 50, 51

Galloway, D. *et al.* 37, 51, 100
Gipps, C. and Stobart, G. 25, 32
Goacher, B. *et al.* 29, 34, 65
governing body, roles and responsibilities 57
graduated model of assessment 35–7
Grant Maintained Schools Act (1996) 2
group education plans (GEPs) 41

headteachers *see* staff
Hegarty, S. 12, 13, 88

identification *see* early identification; labelling
'identity of difference' 50
IEP *see* individual education plan
inclusion
  action plan 58
  barriers to 15–16
  creating cultures of 16–18
  effective education 15
  and integration 11–13
  and LSA 105–6, 110–11
  policy framework 60–5
  policy rationale 53–6
  policy sample 66–71
  practice development 18–19
  practice review 56–60
  process of 12–13
  settings 13–14, 15
  vs segregation models of disability 9–11

individual education plan (IEP) 41–6
  assessment and 35, 38, 39, 40
  emotional difficulties *46*
  learning difficulties *45*
  paperwork 79–80
  role of FBA 107
individualistic model *see* medical model
infants school
  policy example 61
  reception class 24, 29, 30, 38
  see also settings
information
  and involvement of parents 93–4
  policy 60–5, 66–71
integration and inclusion 11–13

Jones, C. 4, 10, 21, 22–4, 29, 77, 79, 80, 98, 102, 103–4

labelling
  LSA 104, 110
  negative aspects 16, 23–4, 26, 38, 50–1
  non-labelling approaches 10–11
  positive aspects 51
  see also early identification
language
  of policy document 54–5
  of SEN 5, *6*, *7*
  see also definitions; models
language difficulties 39
  case example 48–9
leadership/management role, SENCO 75, 81
learning difficulties
  definition 8
  IEP *45*
learning support assistant (LSA) 101–3, 110–11
  flexible budget system 106–9
  inclusion and 105–6, 110–11
  principles for effective practice 103–5
  views 103–4, 105

Lewis, A. 13, 31
  et al. 33, 73, 76, 77, 79
liaison role, SENCO 75, 76, 83
Lindsay, G. 26
  and Desforges, M. 24, 26, 27, 31–2
listening skills 39
Lloyd, C. 113
local education authorities (LEAs) 11,
    33, 34, 73, 78
  partnership 93
  statements 47
  Warwickshire County Council
    (WCC) 74, 106–9
LSA see learning support assistant
Luton, K. 58, 59

Madden, P. 100
mainstream settings 13–14, 57
  SENCO roles 73, 78
  vs special schools, case examples
    48–50
management
  leadership role, SENCO 75, 81
  of paperwork 79–82
Mason, M. 10, 110–11
medical model 9–10, 11, 16, 22
medical profession see professional(s)
models
  disability 9–11
  graduated assessment 35–7
  partnership 89–92
Moyles, J. 101

National Association for Special
  Educational Needs (NASEN) 103,
  104, 105
National Curriculum 2, 25, 31
National Standards for Special Education
  Needs Coordinators (TTA) 80–1
National Standards for Under Eights
  Daycare and Childminding (DfES) 2
negotiating model of partnership 91–2
non-contact role, LSA 102, 103
non-labelling approaches 10–11
non-LEA maintained sector, SENCO
  roles 73–4

Nursery Education: Desirable Outcomes
  for Children's Learning on Entering
  Compulsory Education (SCAA) 2
nursery school/preschool groups
  assessment 29–30, 34, 38, 48
  examples 48–50
  flexible budget scheme 106
  policy examples 55, 60–1, 63, 64,
    66–71
  SENCO roles 73, 77–8

obstructive model of partnership 90
Office for Standards in Education
  (Ofsted) 53–4, 55
outside agencies see external agencies

Papatheodorou, T. et al. 102–3, 105–6
paperwork see administrative role,
  SENCO
parents
  in assessment 30, 34, 40, 47, 54
  consent 25, 40, 47, 93–4
  in decision-making 54
  definition 86–7
  in Early Years Action 38
  and SEN policy 55
  views 94, 100
  see also partnership
partnership 86–8, 99–100
  creating inclusive cultures 16–18
  definition 88–9
  models 89–92
  policy framework 64–5
  in practice 92–9
  see also parents
physical barriers to inclusion 15–16
physical impairments assessment 47–8
Plowden Report 87
policy initiatives 1–4
  see also Code of Practice (DfE/DfES);
    inclusion; Warnock Report; and
    specific departments/publications
political aspects of assessment 32, 34–5
political barriers to inclusion 16
Portage scheme 90–1

preschool groups *see* nursery schools
preschool networks 64–5
primary school
  policy example 62
  see also settings
professional(s) 25, 37
  judgements/perceptions 34–5, 37,
    48–50
  see also partnership; staff

Qualifications and Curriculum
  Authority (QCA) 1, 3
qualifications, FBA 107

reception class 24, 29, 30, 38
record keeping 79, 80
  see also administrative role, SENCO
recruitment and retention, FBA 108–9
referral 37, 79
resistance to inclusion 16
rights of the child 98
Roffey, S. 25
Rusteimer, S. and Shaw, L. 101, 110–11

'School Action' 37, 41
'School Action Plus' 37, 41
School Curriculum and Assessment
  Authority (SCAA) 2
School Standards and Framework Act
  (1998) 2
schools *see* settings; *specific types*
segregation 12, 16
  vs inclusion models of disability
    9–11
SEN Programme of Action (DfEE) 99
SEN register 38, 50
SEN Toolkit (DfES) 37, 99
'The SENCO Guide' 78
setting managers 37, 57
settings
  assessments 29, 30
  inclusion 13–14, 15
  policy examples 55, 60–1, 62, 63, 64,
    66–71
  and SENCO roles 72–4

transition between 38
see also specific types
Simmons, K. 72
SMART target 42
social models of disability 10–11
social skills 39
Soder, M. 10–11
special educational needs coordinator
    (SENCO) 72–85, 113
  Code of Practice (DfE/DfES) 72–4, 75–
    6, 78, 79, 83, 84–5
  development needs 80–1, *82*
  and graduated model 37, 38, 39–40,
    41
  key outcomes 83–4
  key responsibilities 74–5
  policy issues 55–6, *57*, 62
  skills and knowledge 80–2
  time management 76–8
  towards effective practice 83
  views 76–8, 80
Special Educational Needs and
    Disability Act (SENDA) (2001) 3
special educational provision,
    definition 8–9
special facilities 62
staff
  communication between 75, 76, 83,
    103–4
  Early Years Action 38
  policy issues 55–6, *57*, 64–5
  views 22–4, 29–30, 105, 106
  see also learning support assistant
    (LSA); special educational needs
    coordinator (SENCO)
statements 47–8
summative assessment 31–2
support, through partnership 94–9

targets
  IEP 42–4
  policy 60
Taylor Report 87
Teacher Training Agency (TTA) 80–1
Ten Reasons for Inclusion 20

terminology *see* definitions; language; models

time management, SENCO 76–8

Tomlinson, S. 5, 9, 33, 51
    Barton, L. and 9

training, FBA 107

transition between settings 38

transplant model of partnership 90–1

UN Convention on the Rights of the Child 98

Warnock Report (DES) 1, 5–6, 7–8, 11, 34, 35, *36*, 87–8, 101

Warwickshire County Council (WCC) 74, 106–9

Weatherley, R. 100

Withers, R. and Lee, J. 34–5

'within child' model *see* medical model

Wolfendale, S. 26, 88, 89, 91, 99

written information 93, 94

written policy 52

written statement 47–8